This Unicorn Coloring Book Belongs To:

____

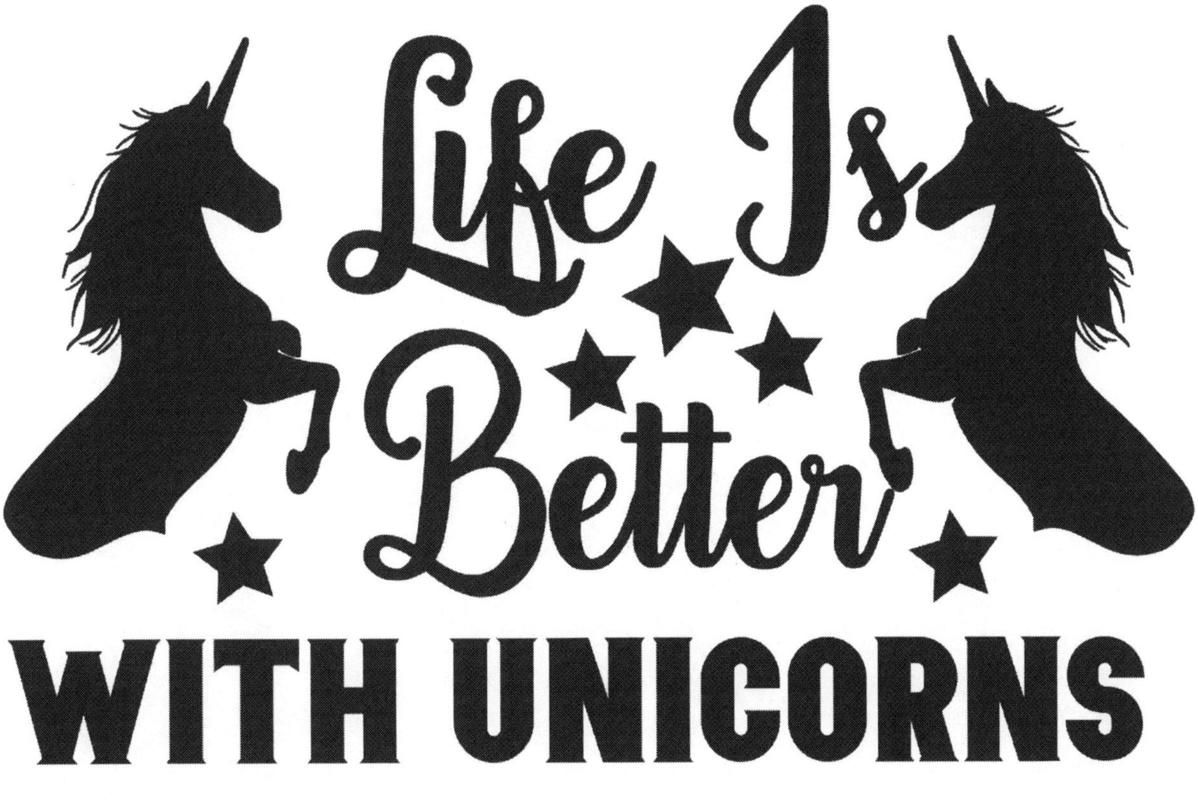

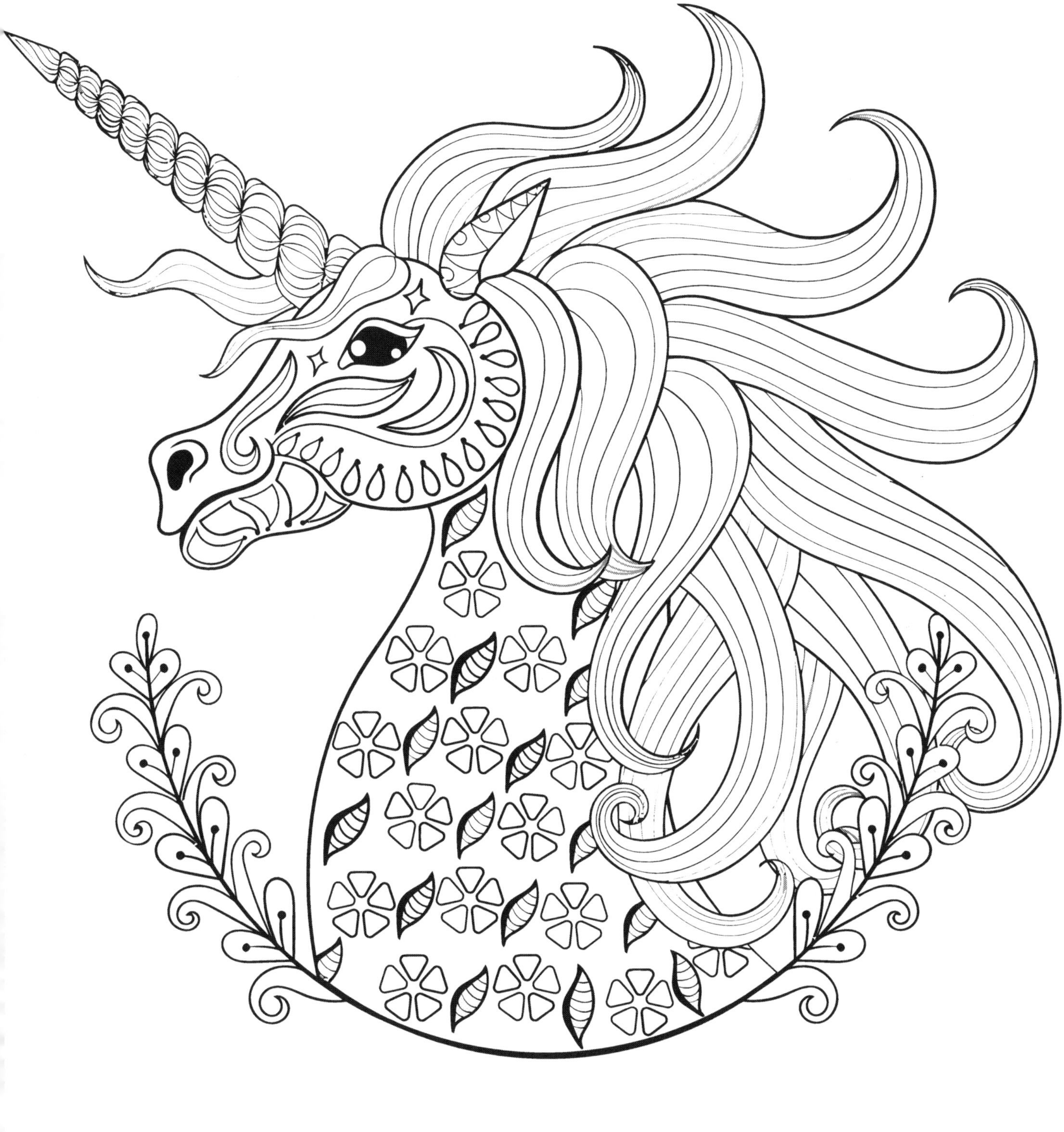

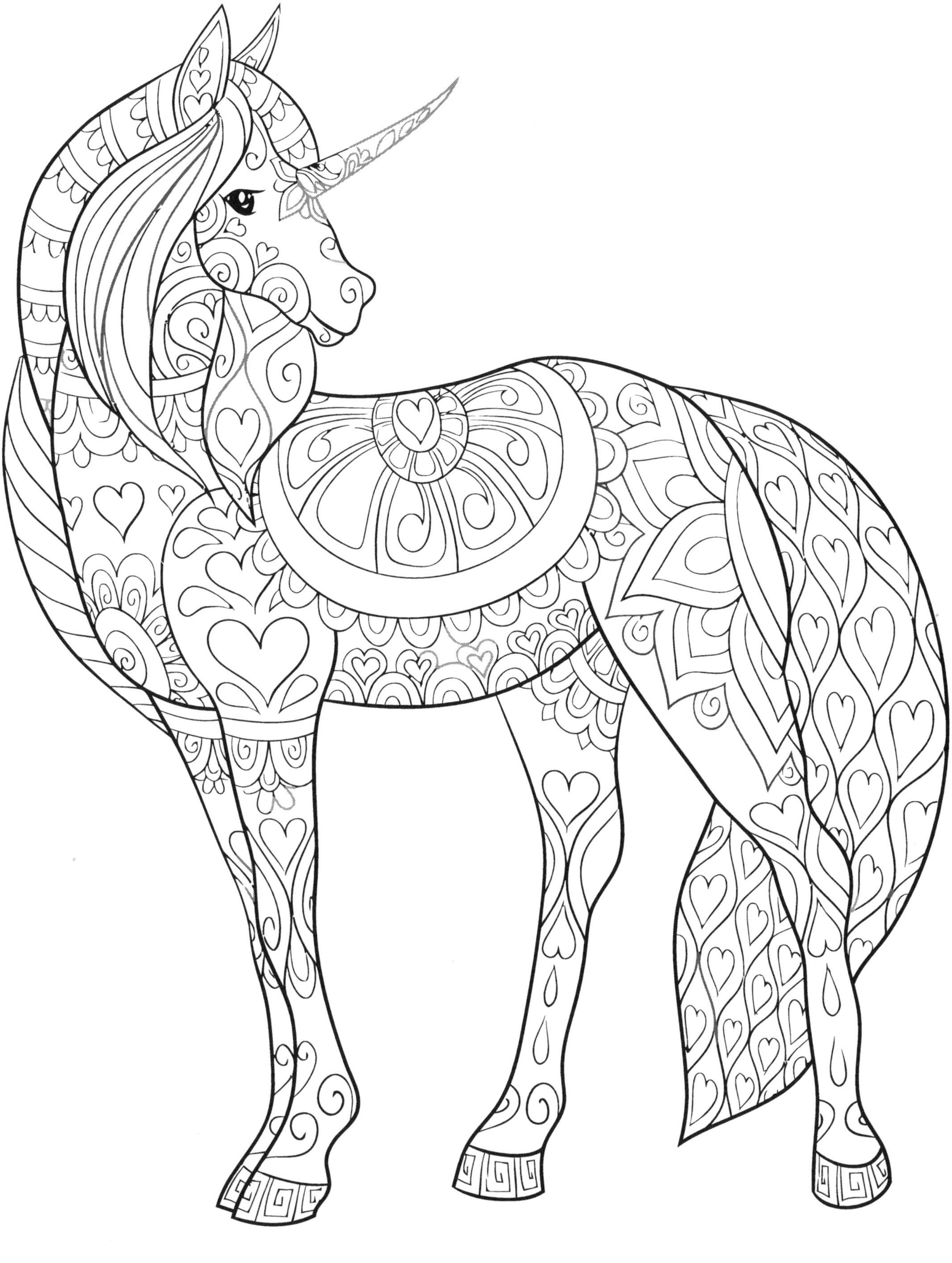

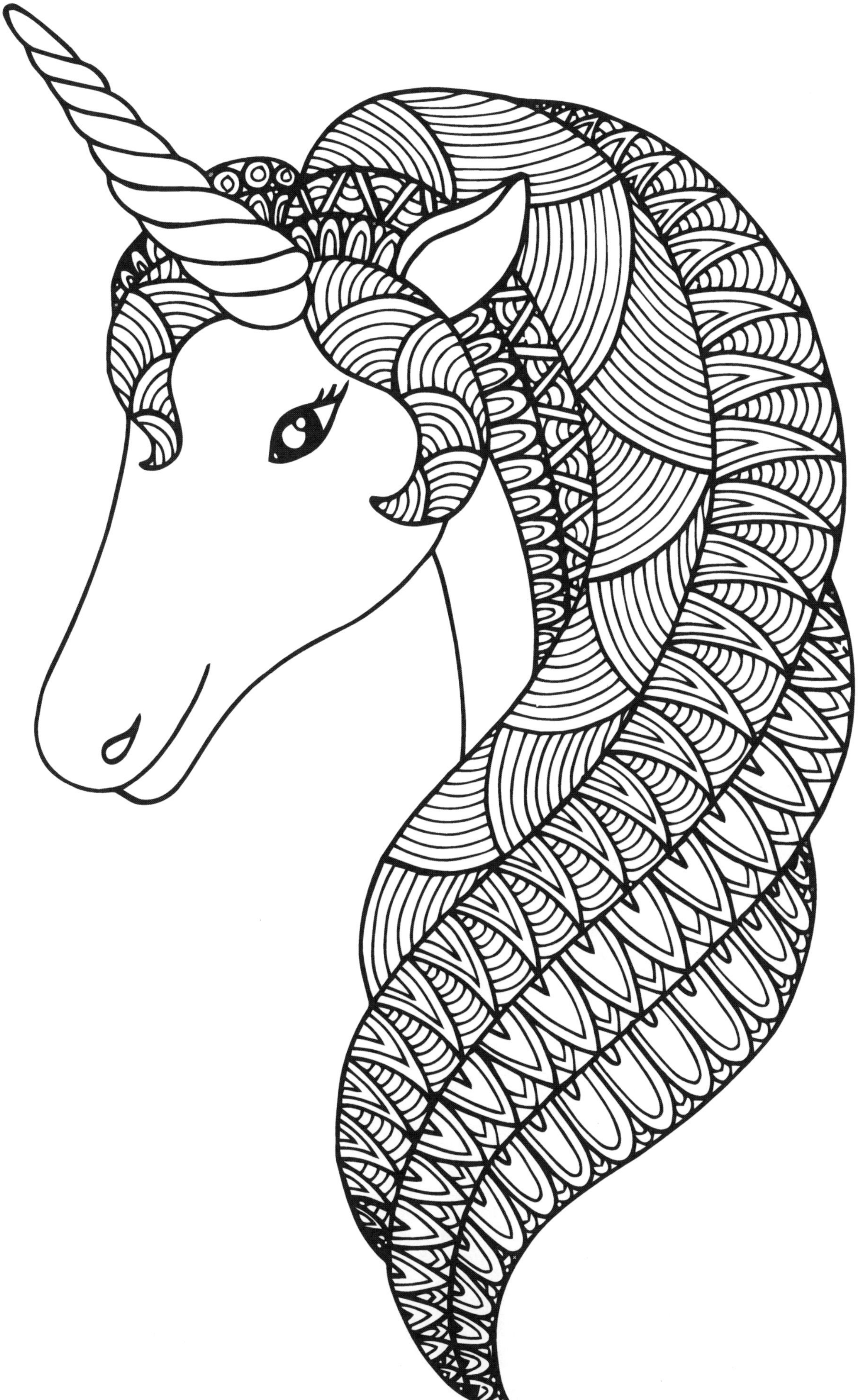

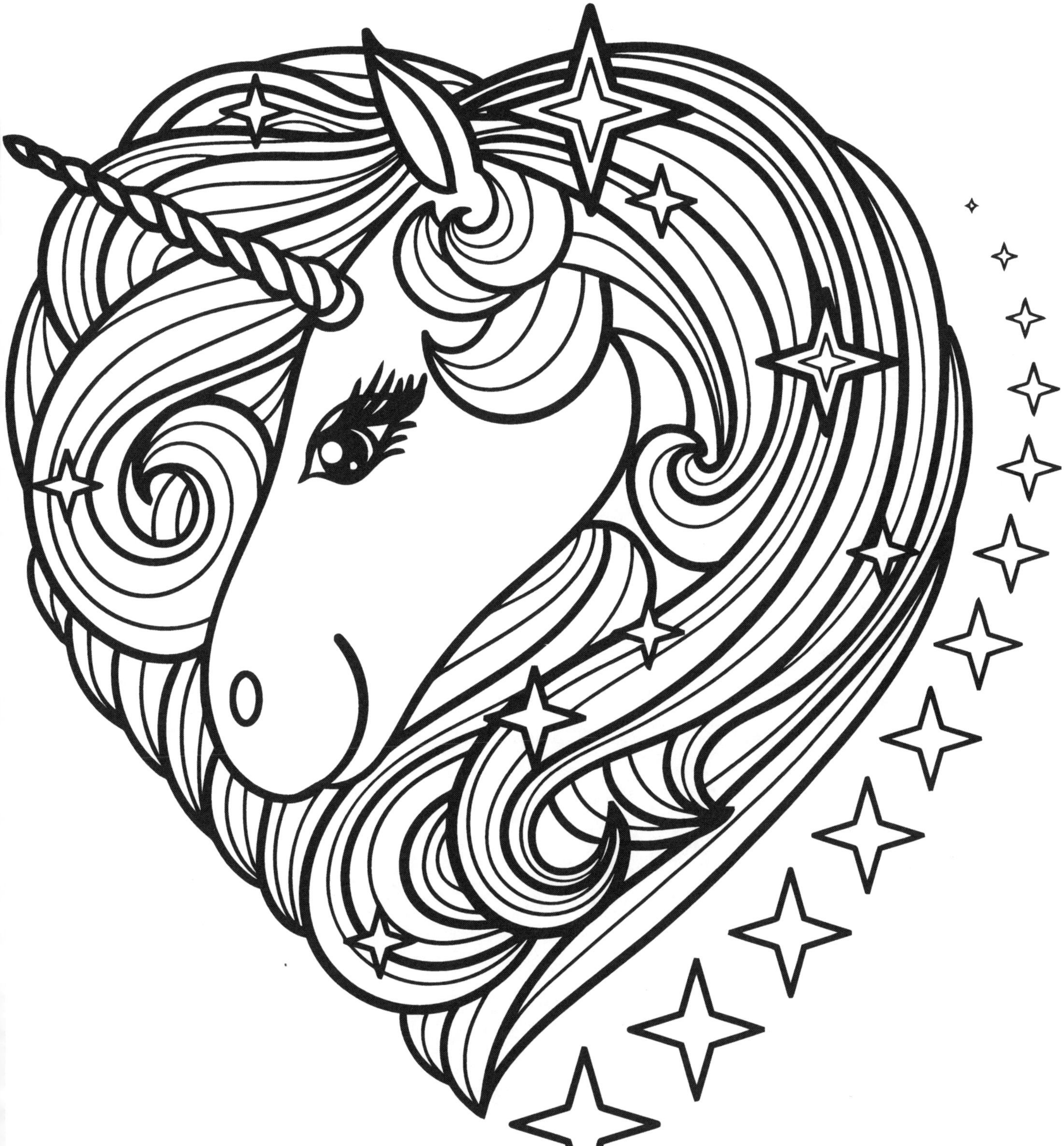

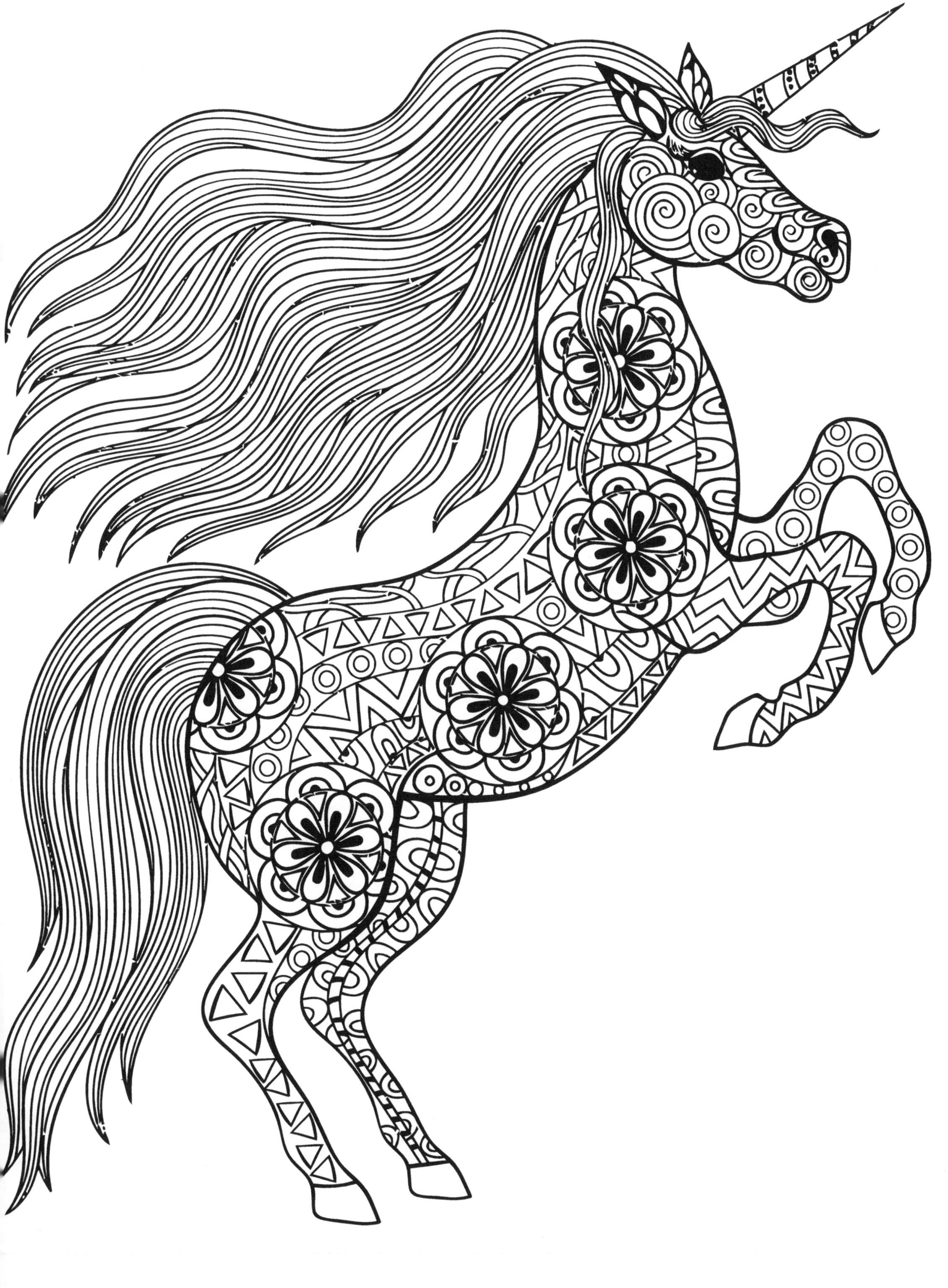

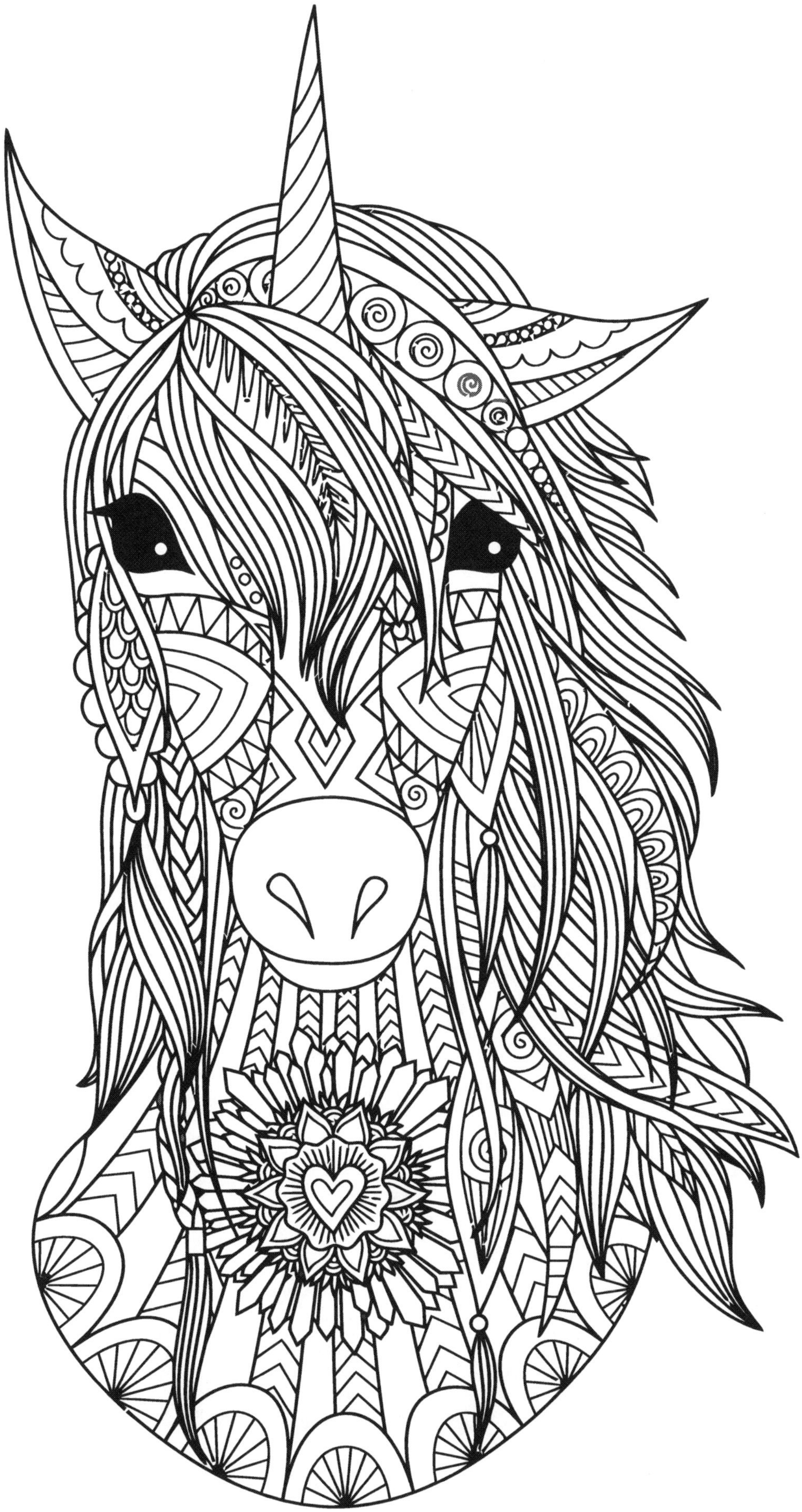

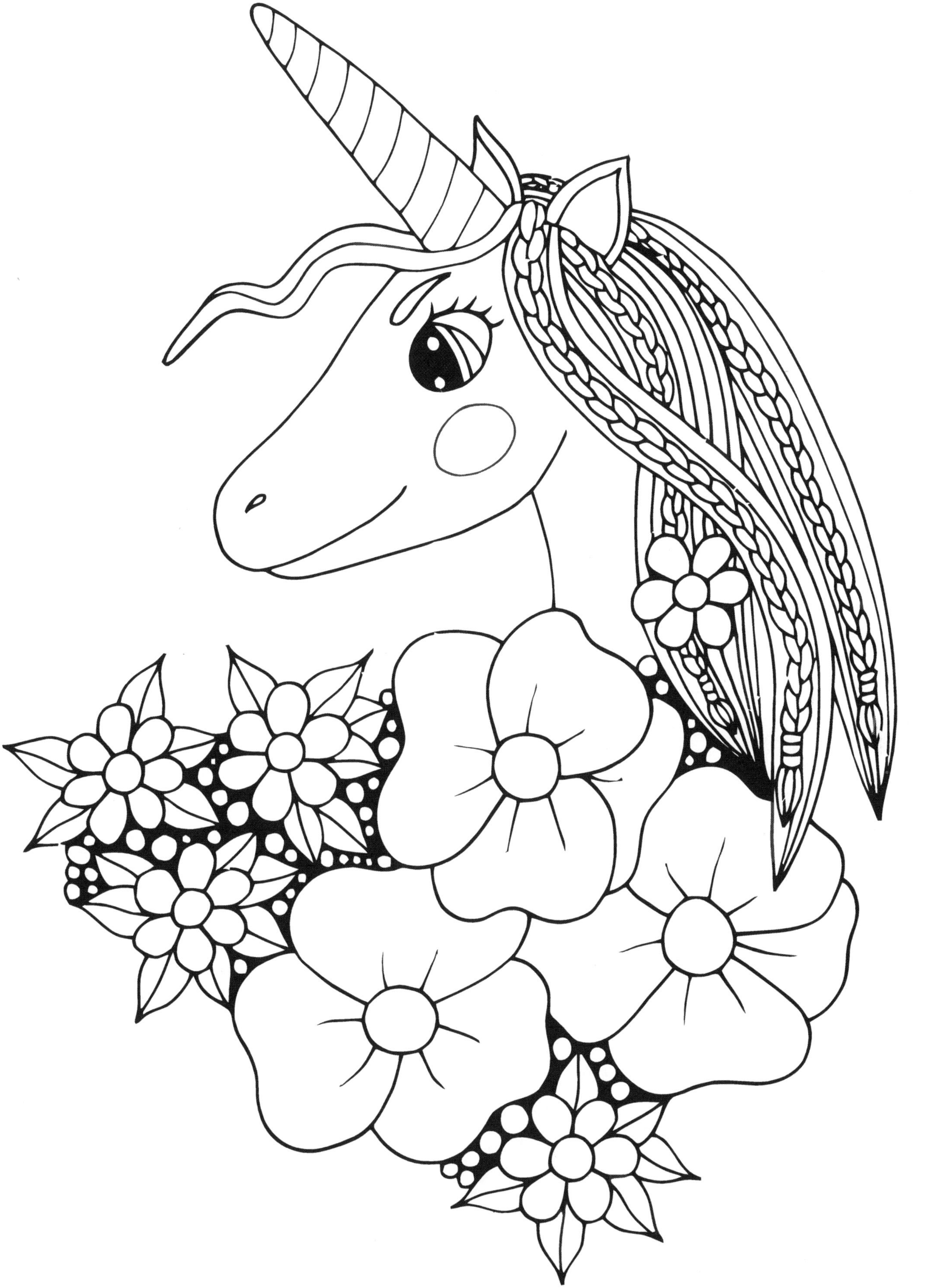

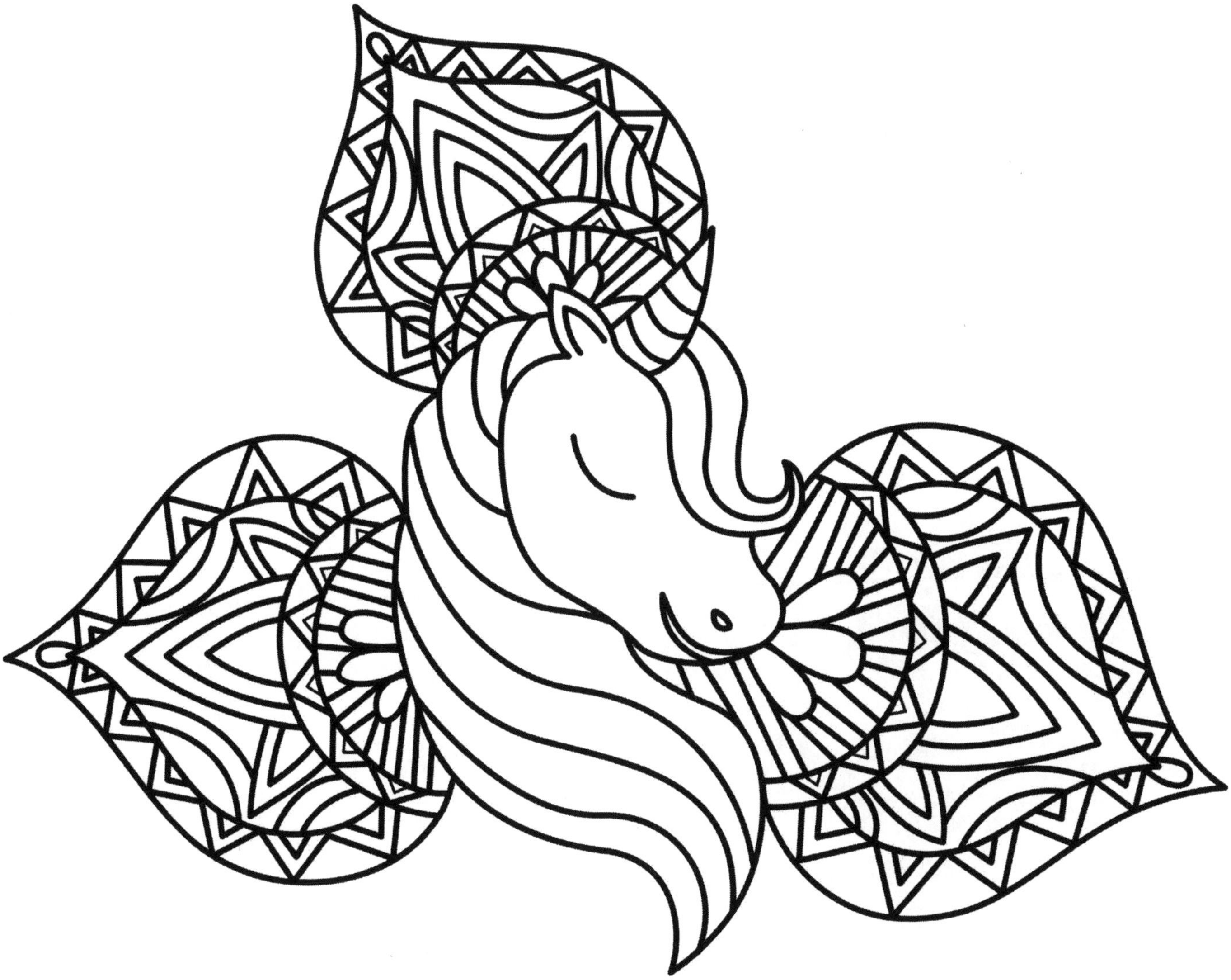

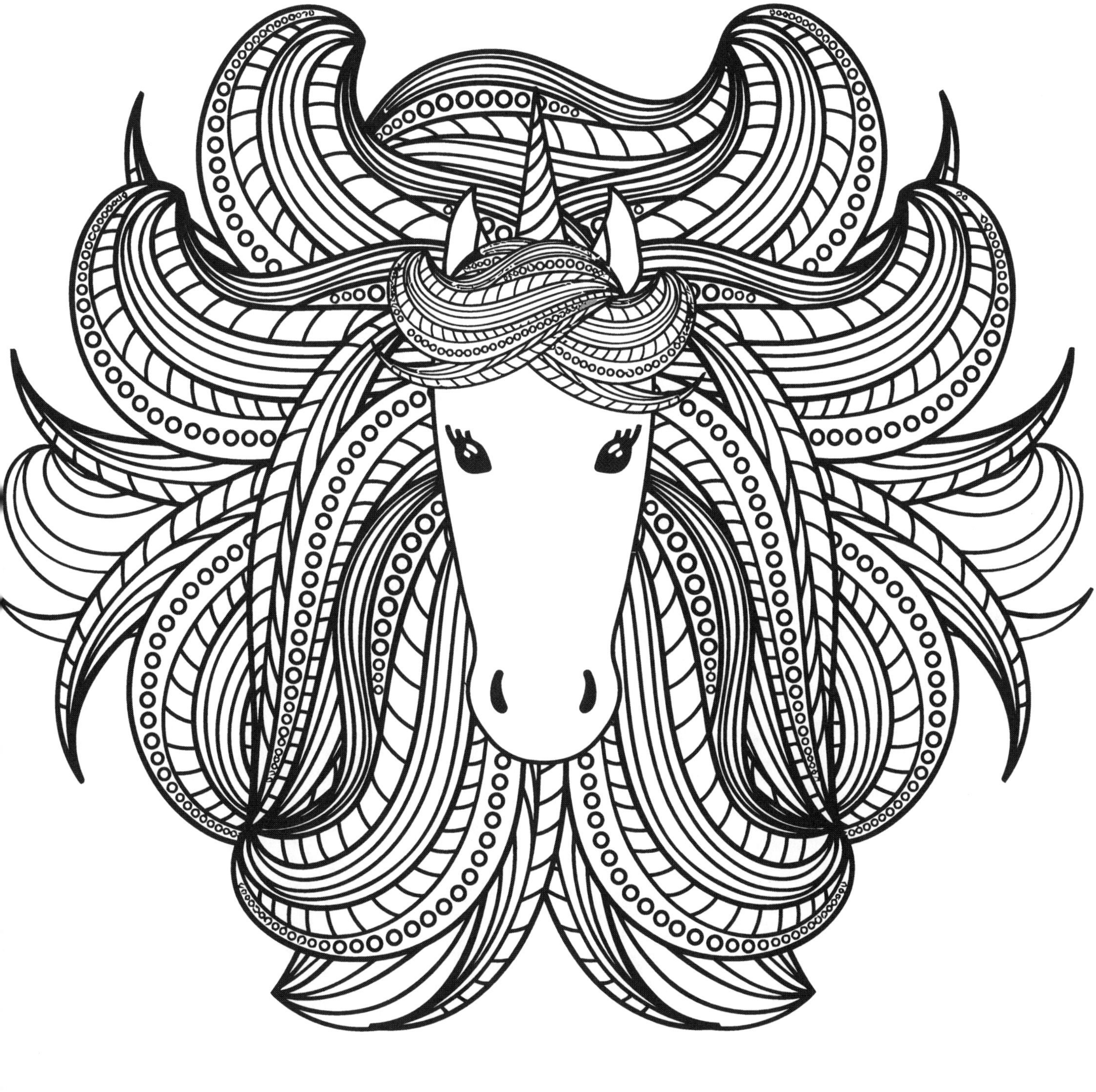

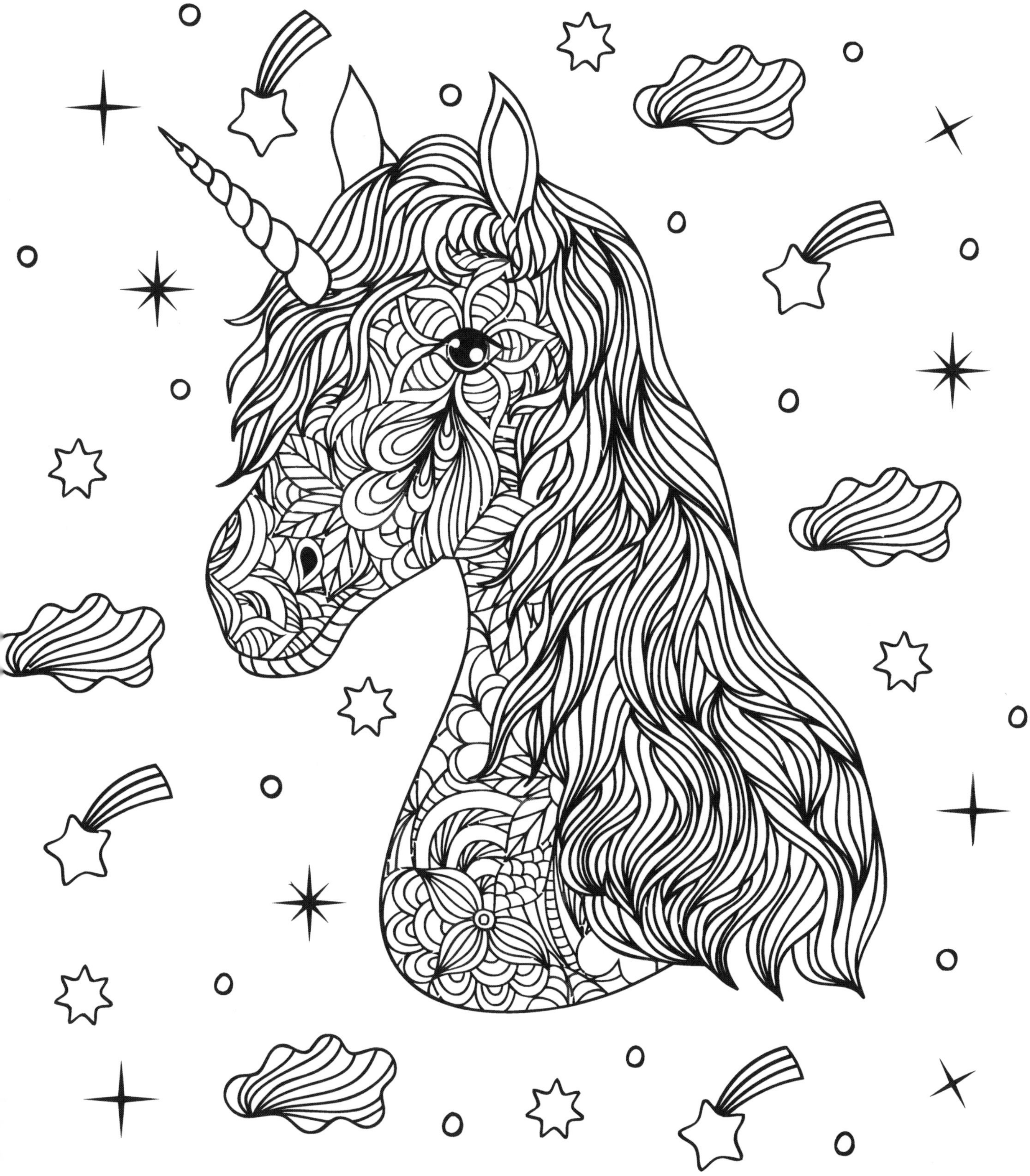

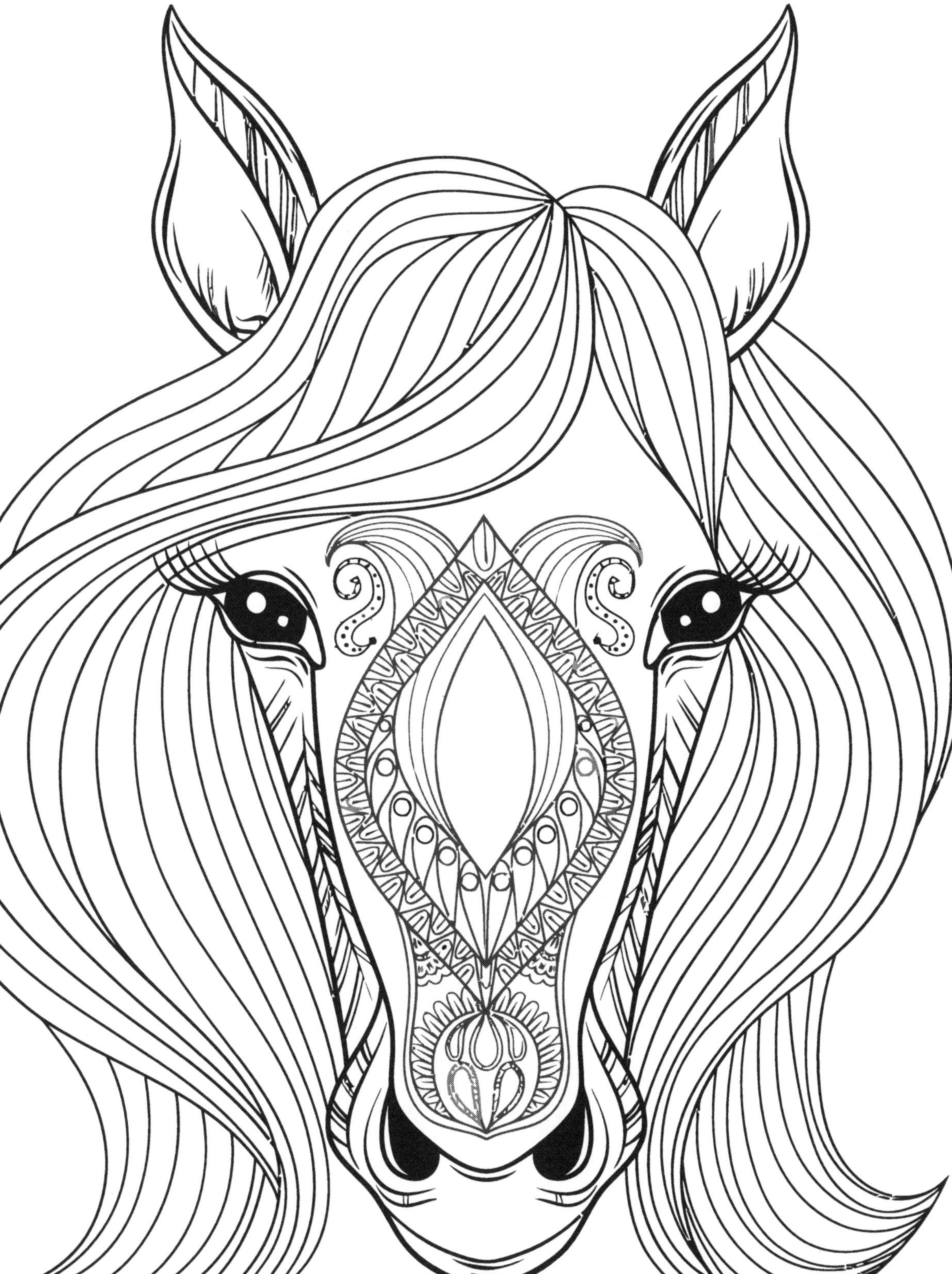

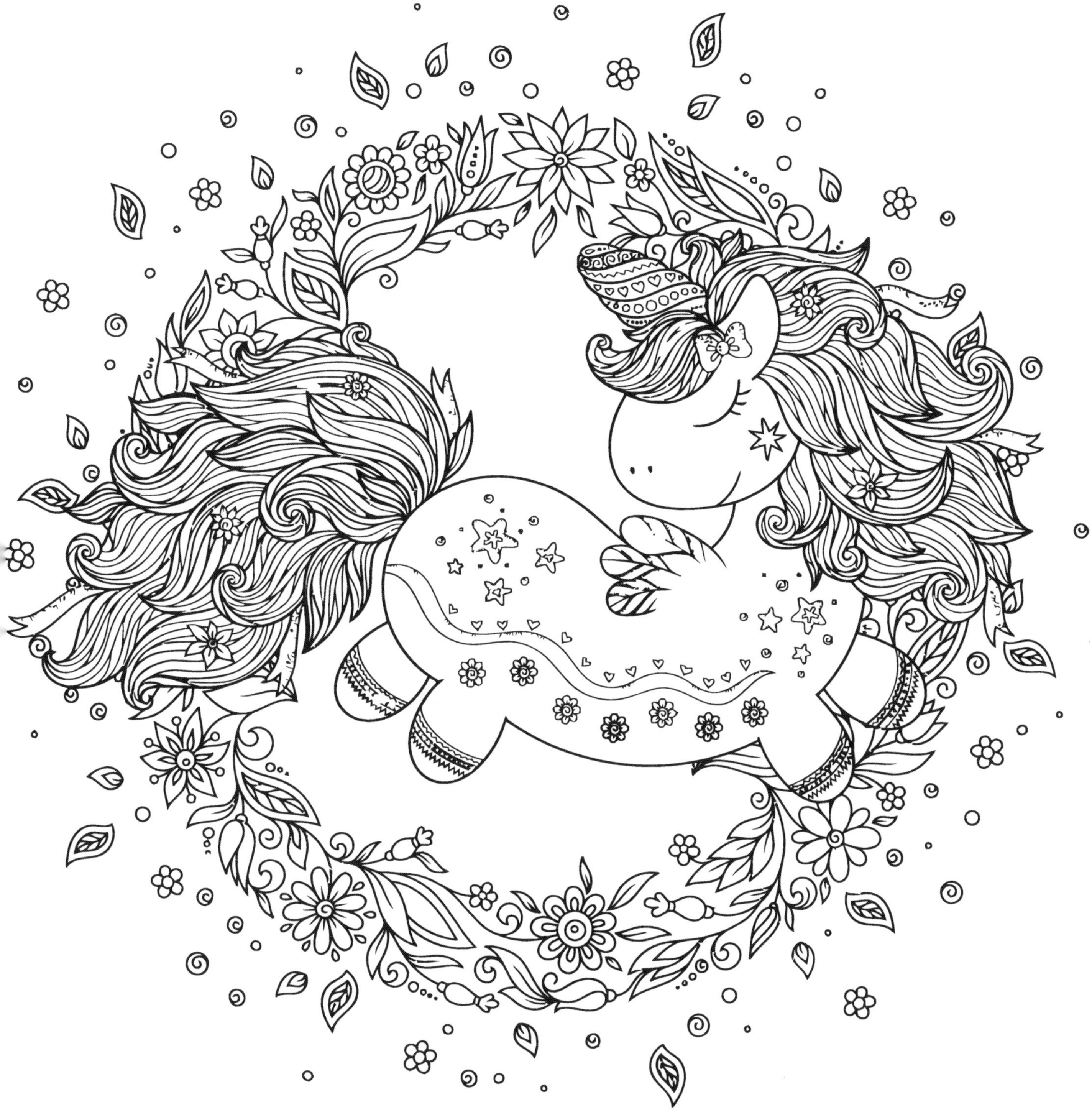

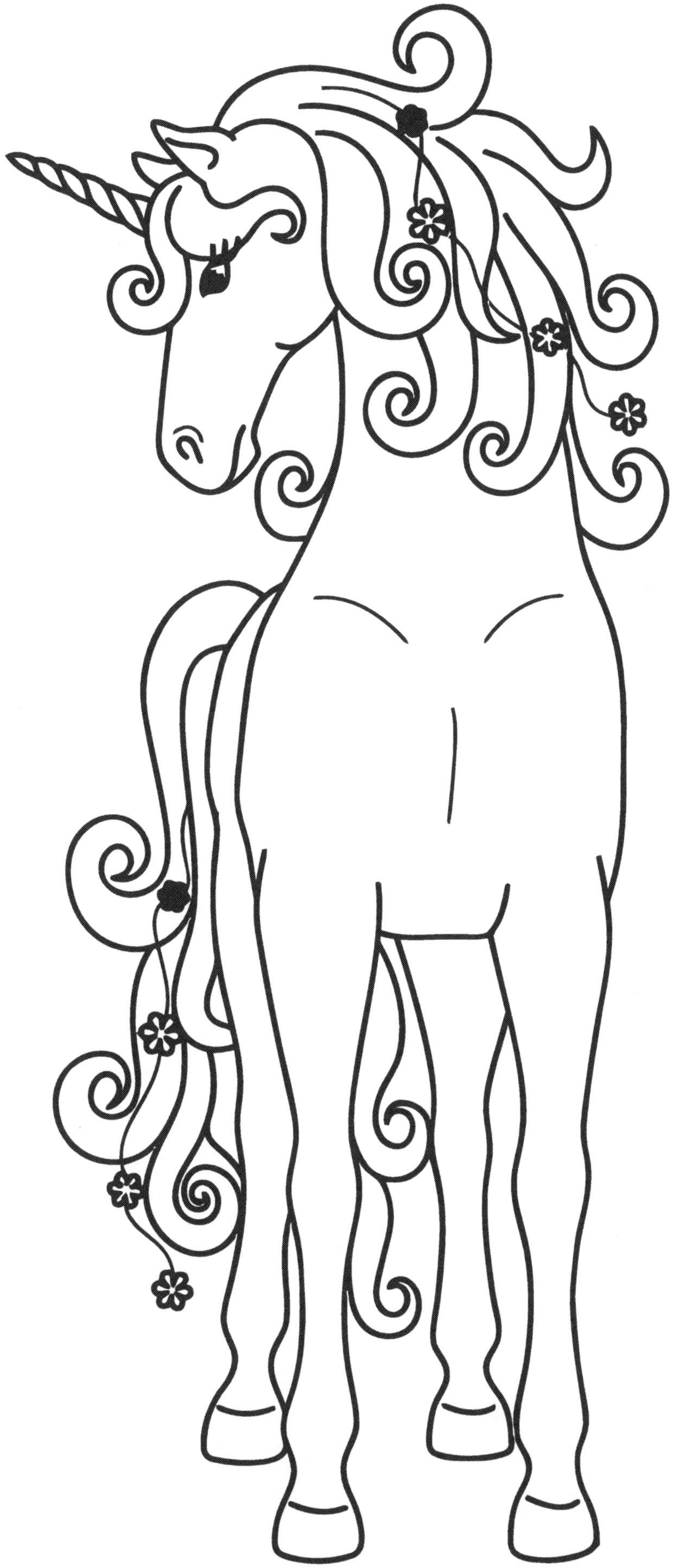

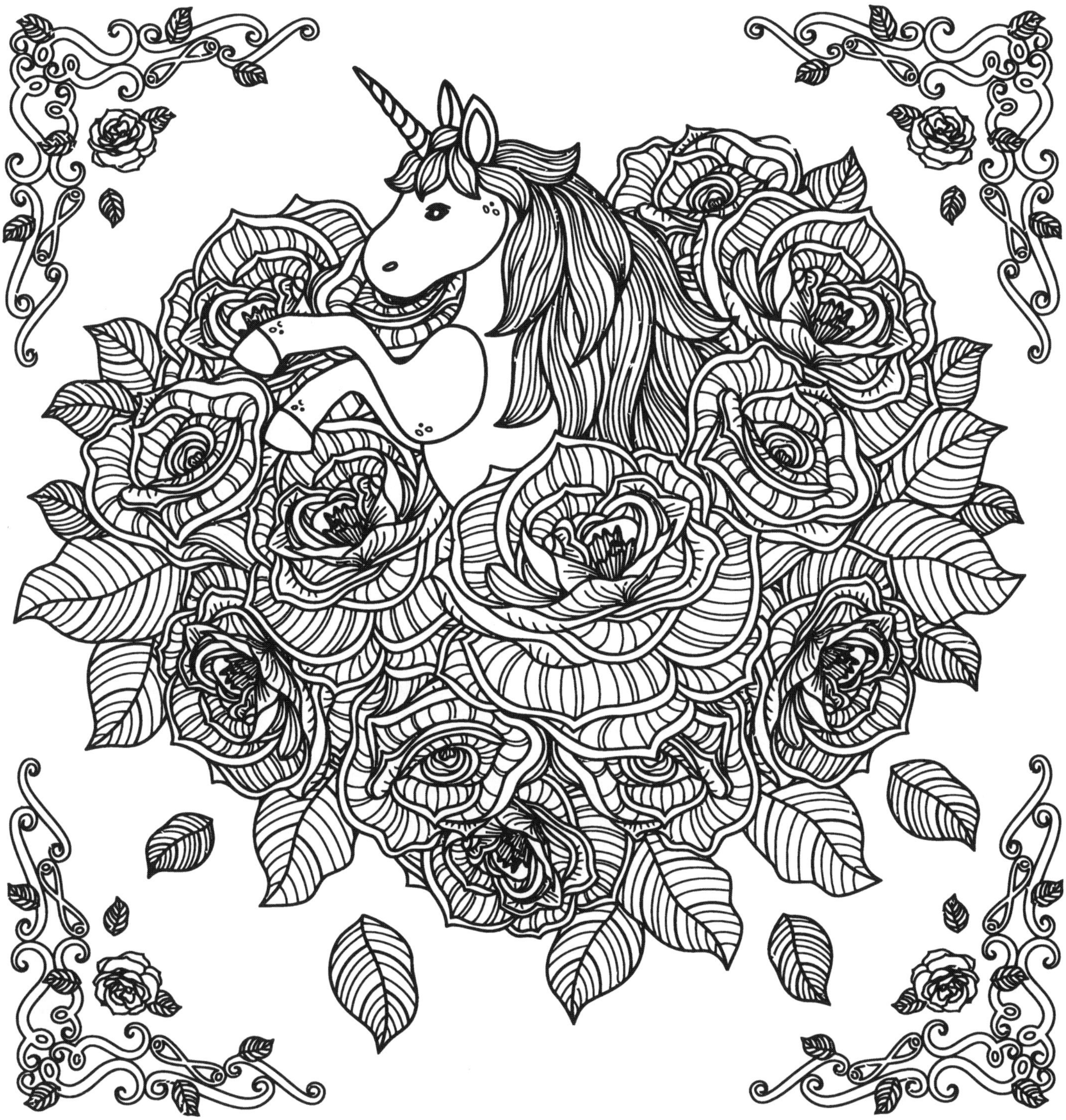

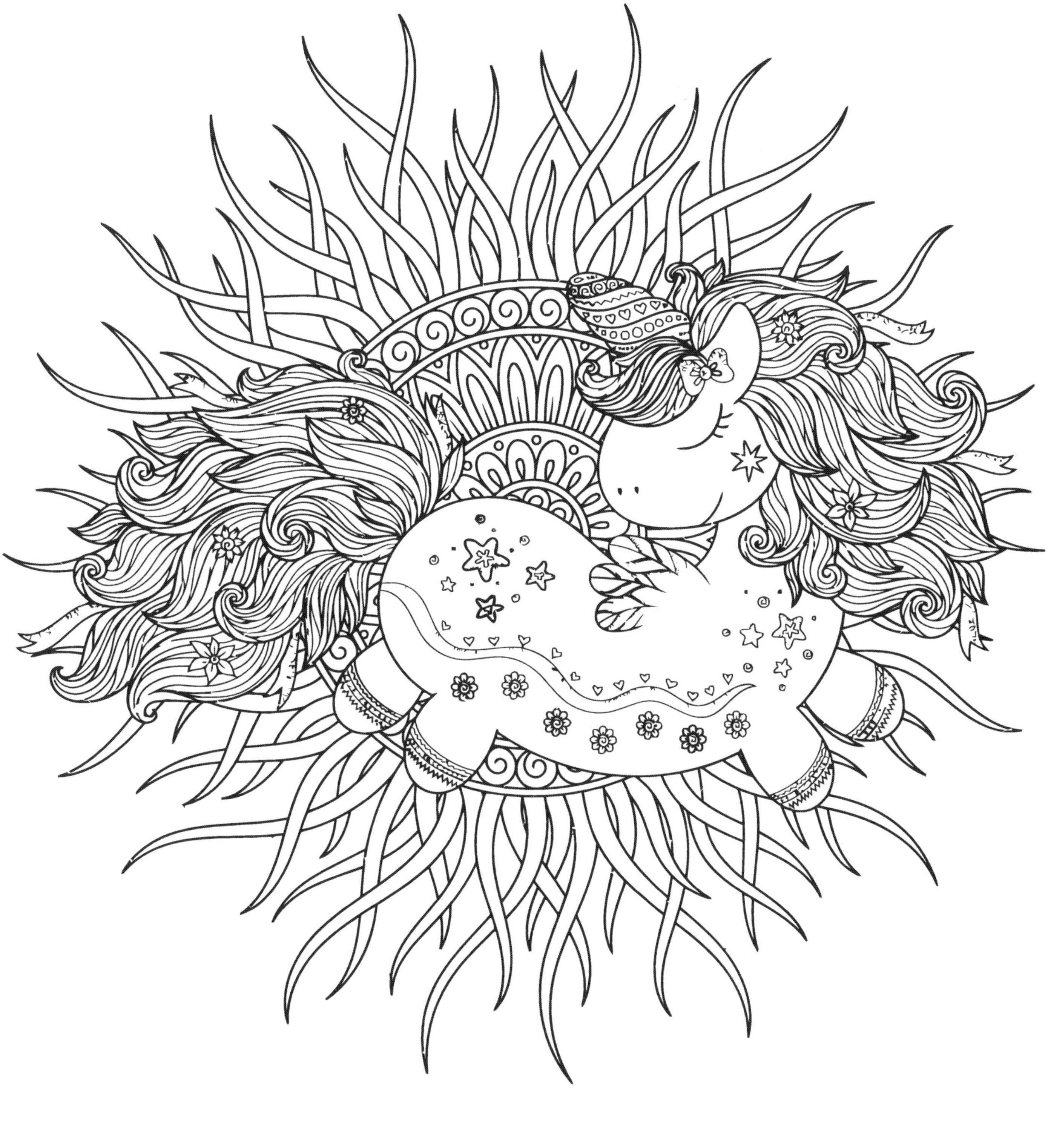

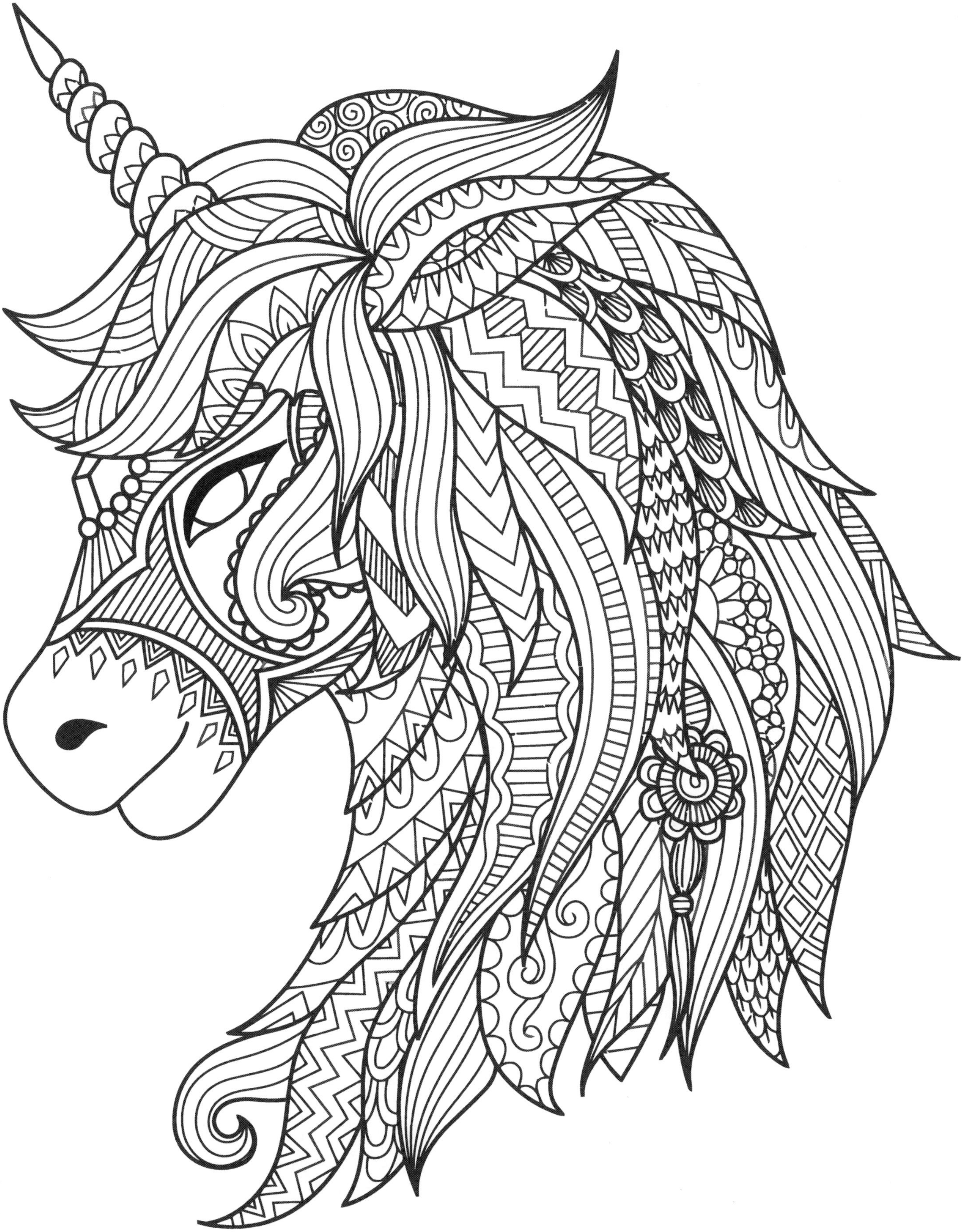

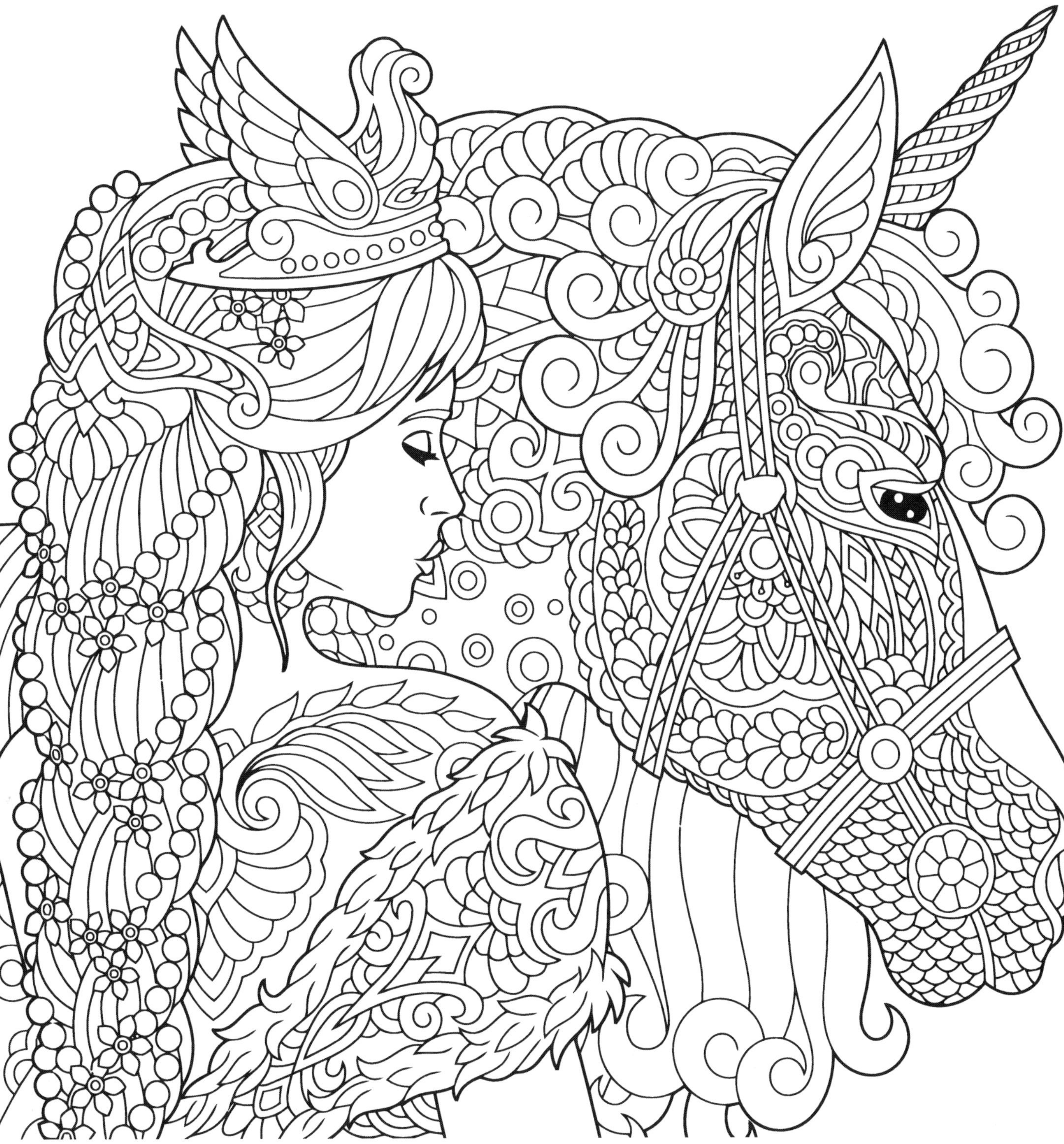

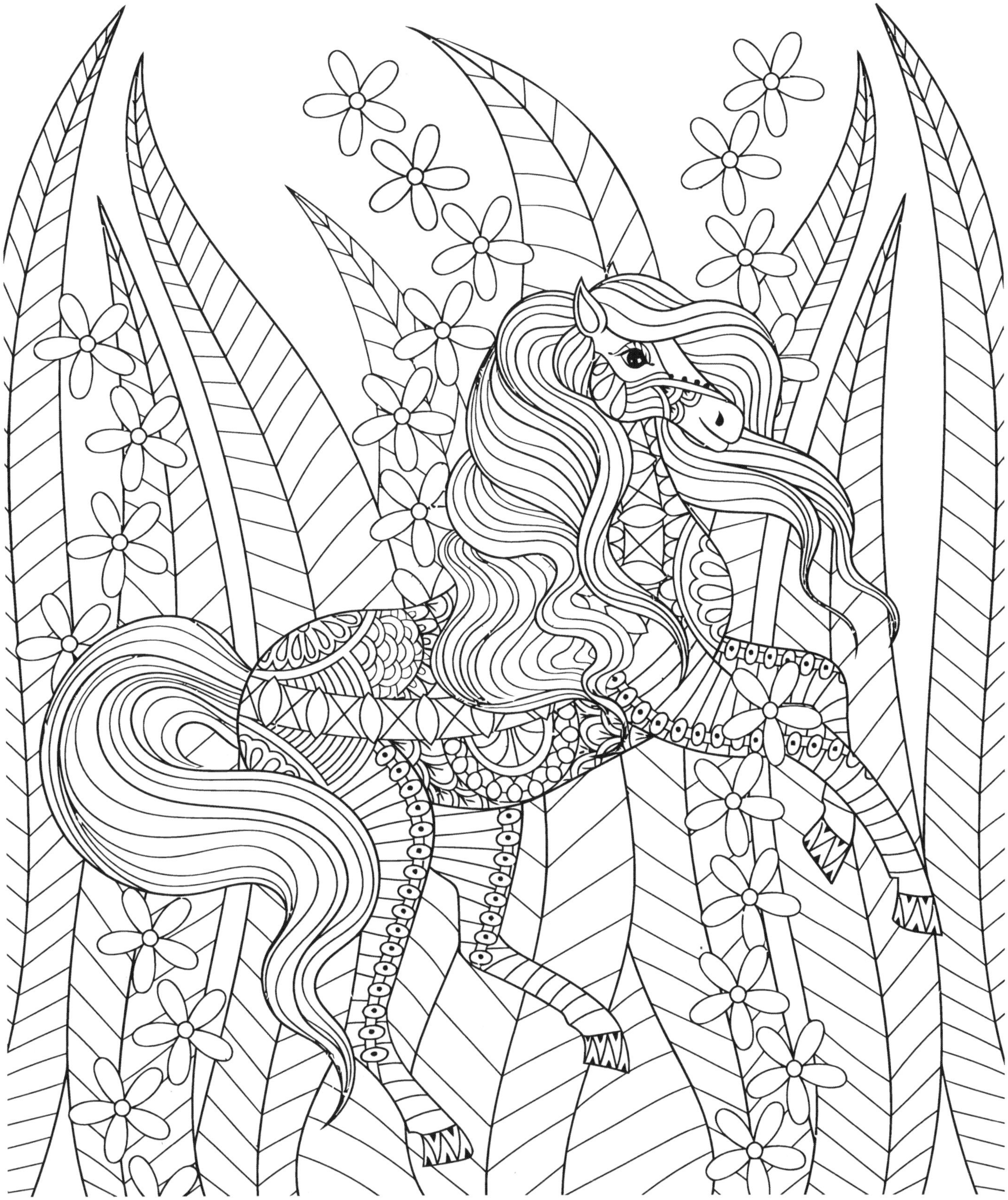

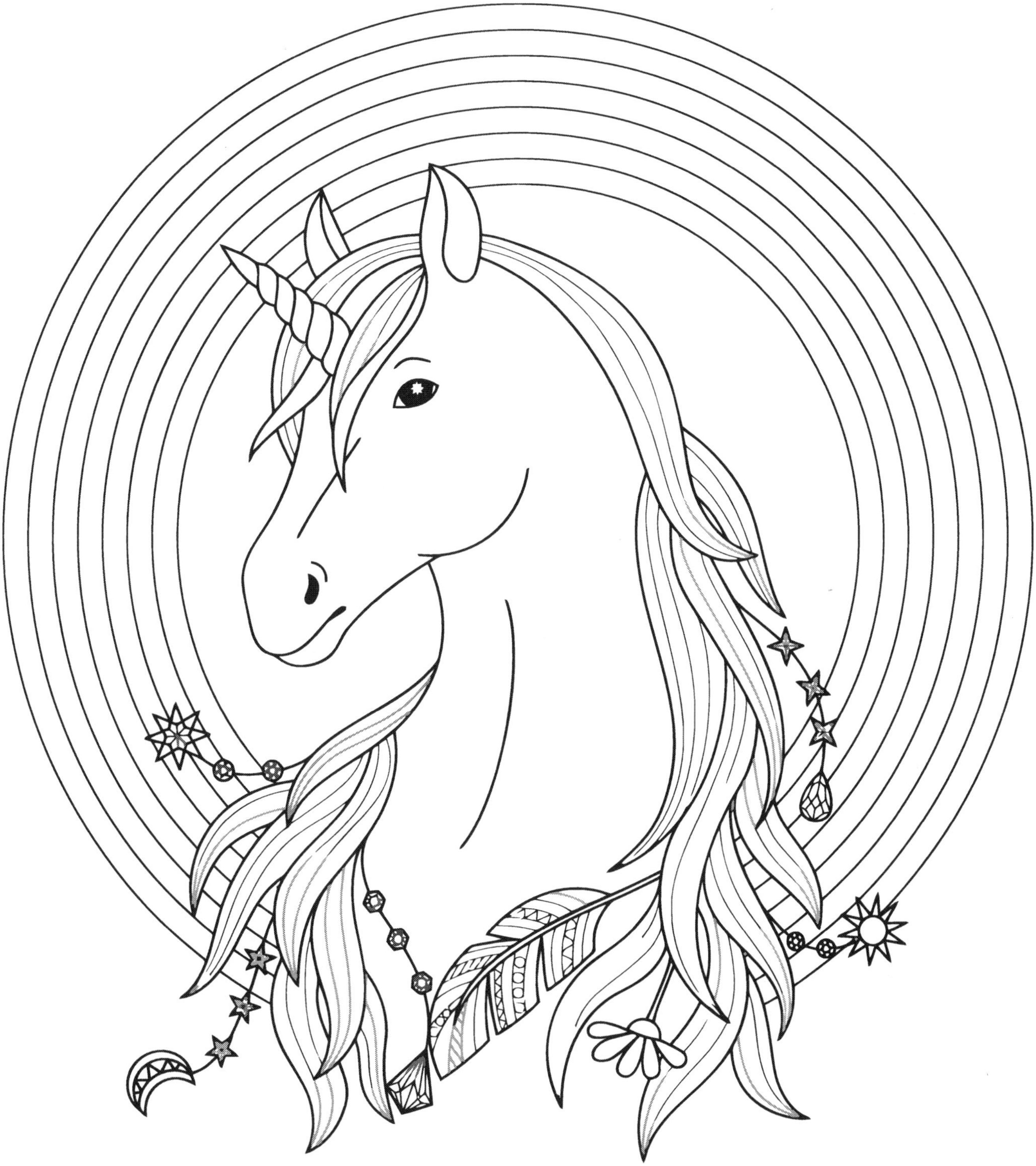

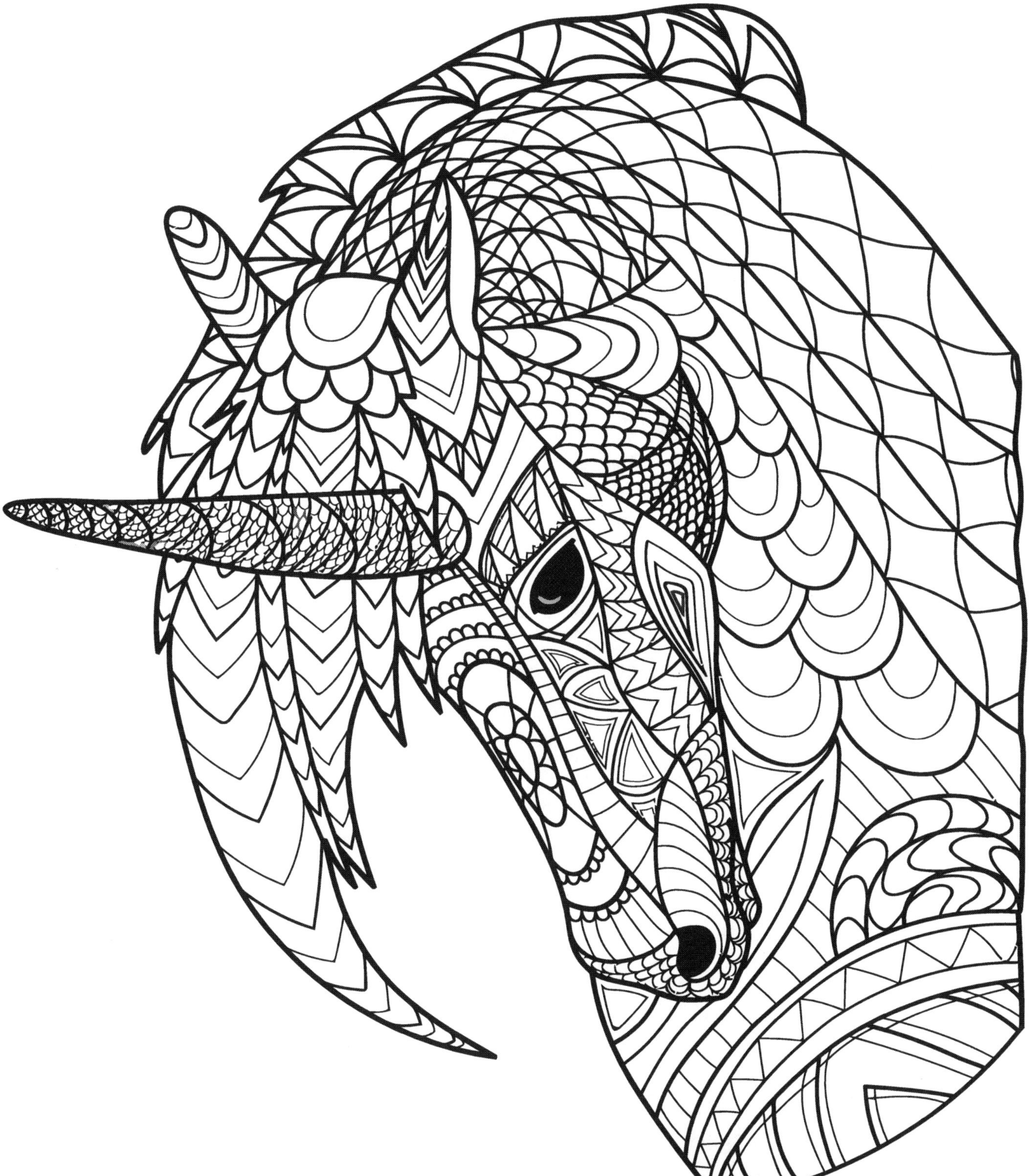

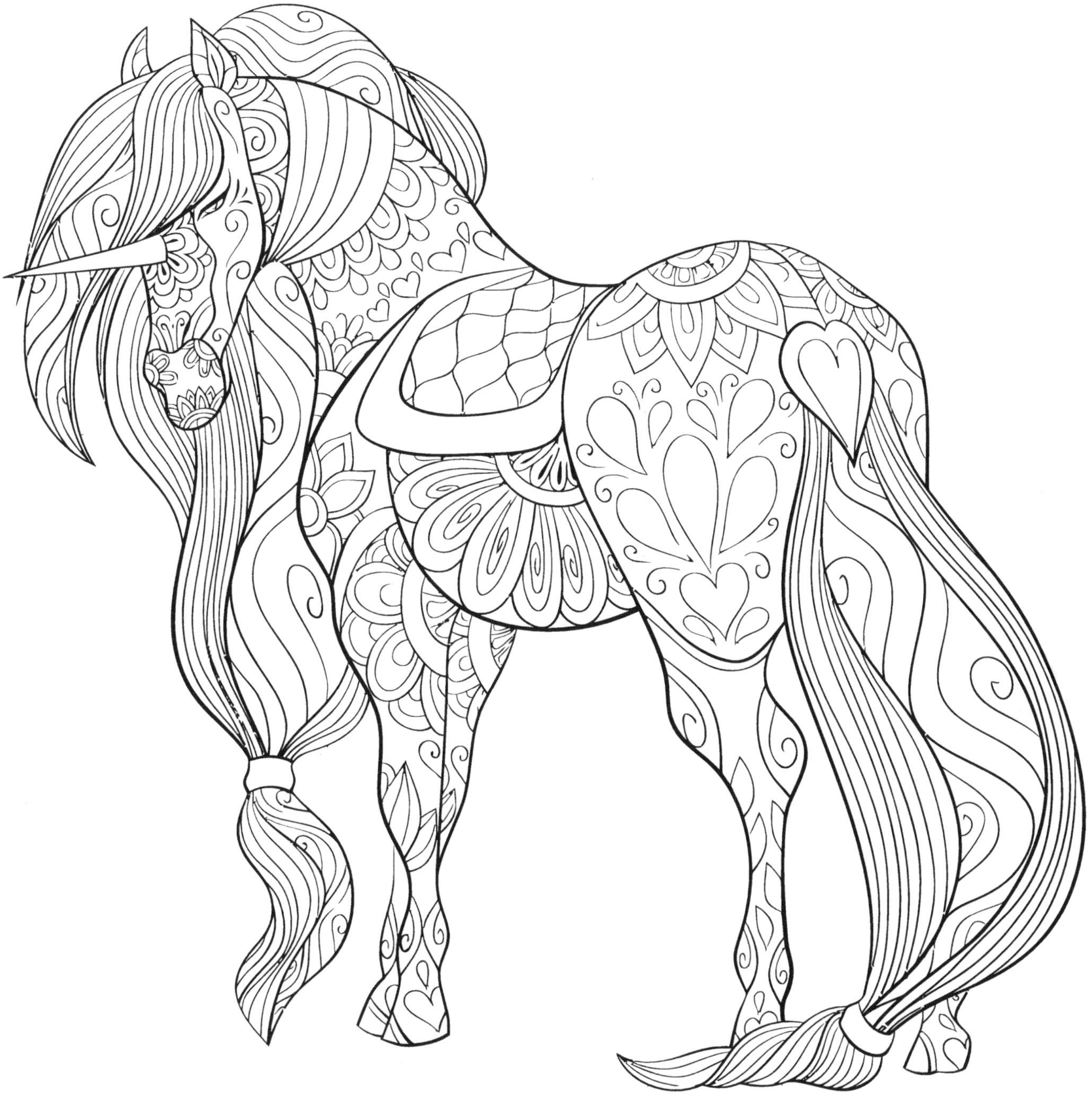

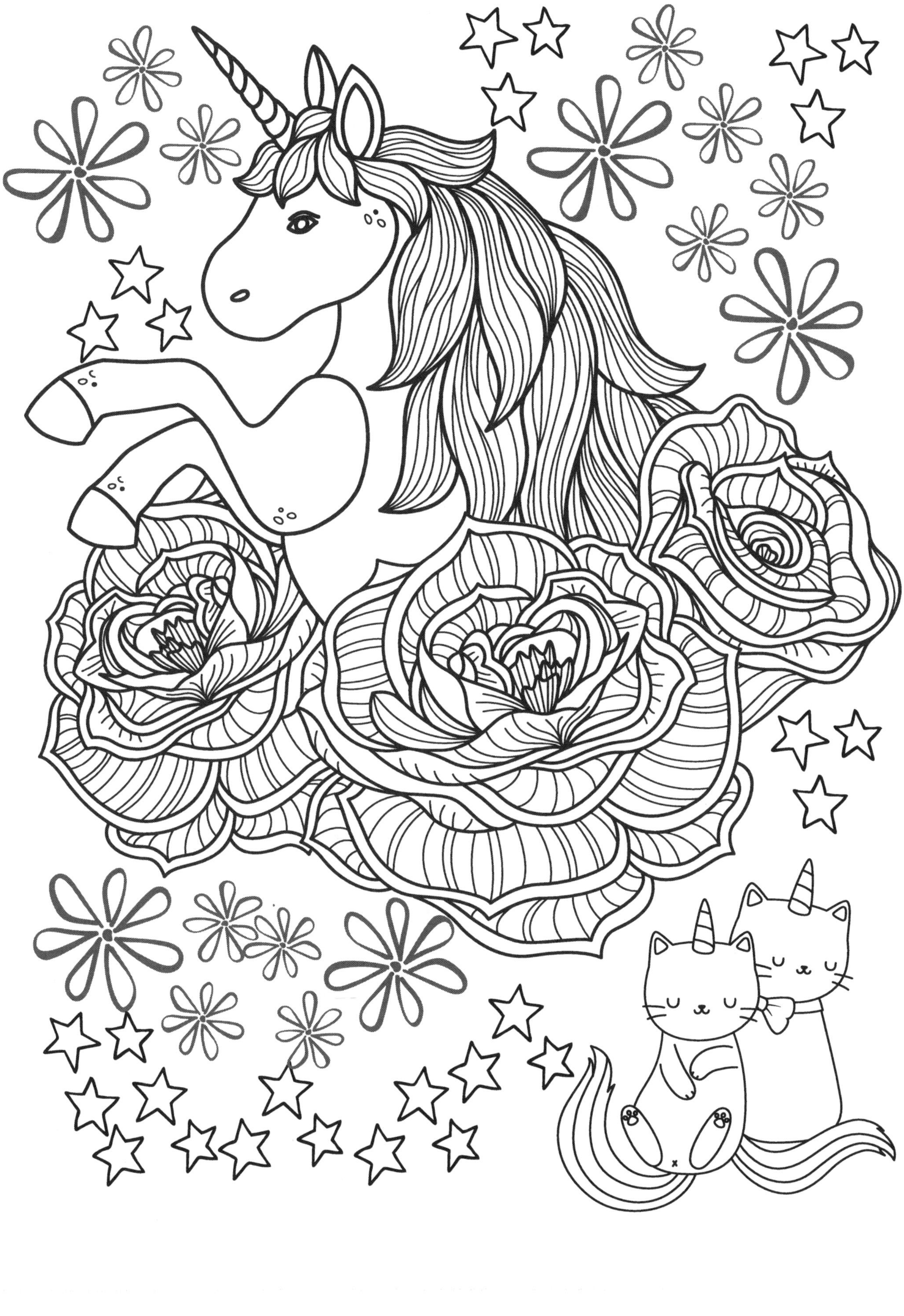

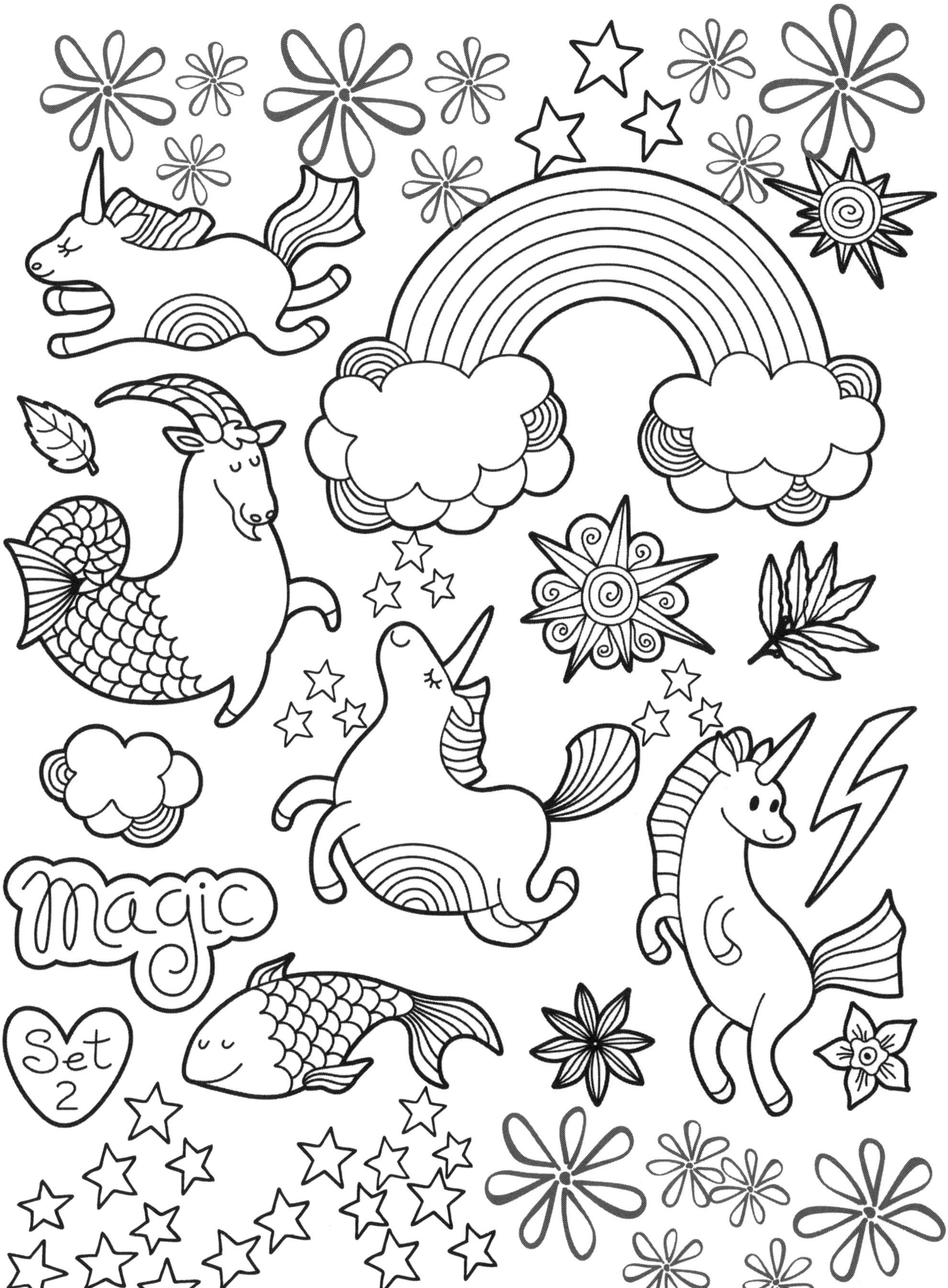
Magic
Set 2

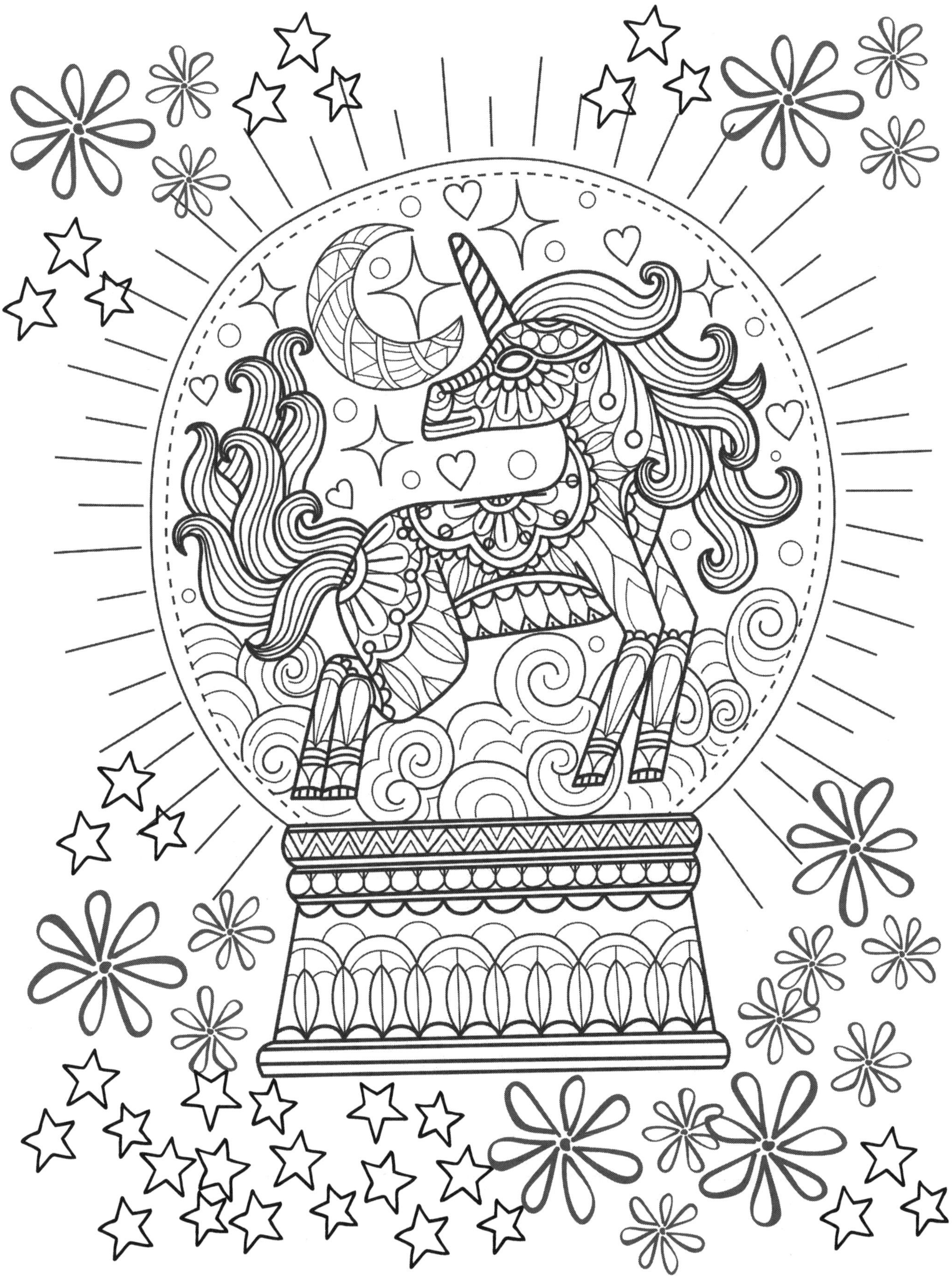

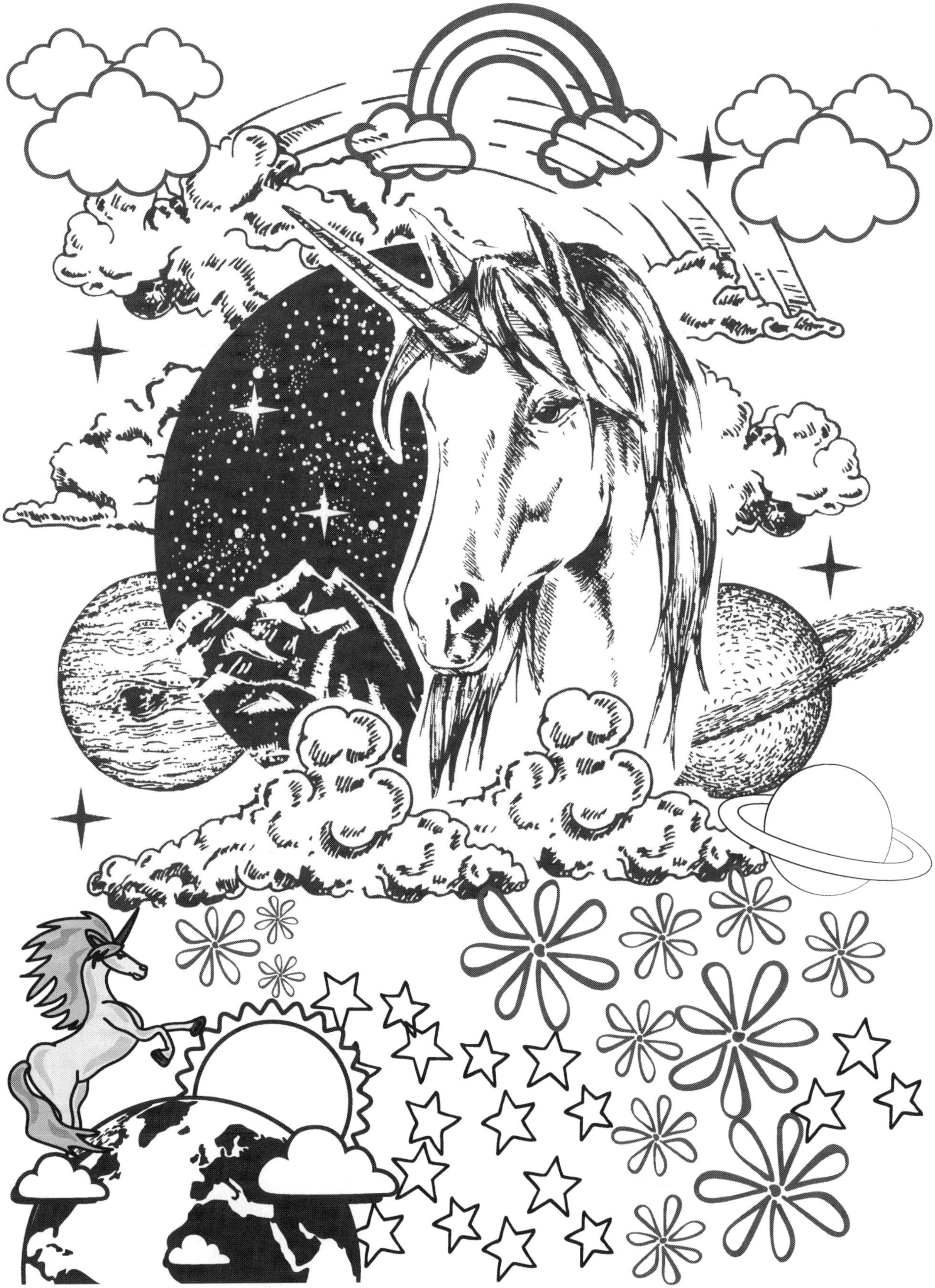

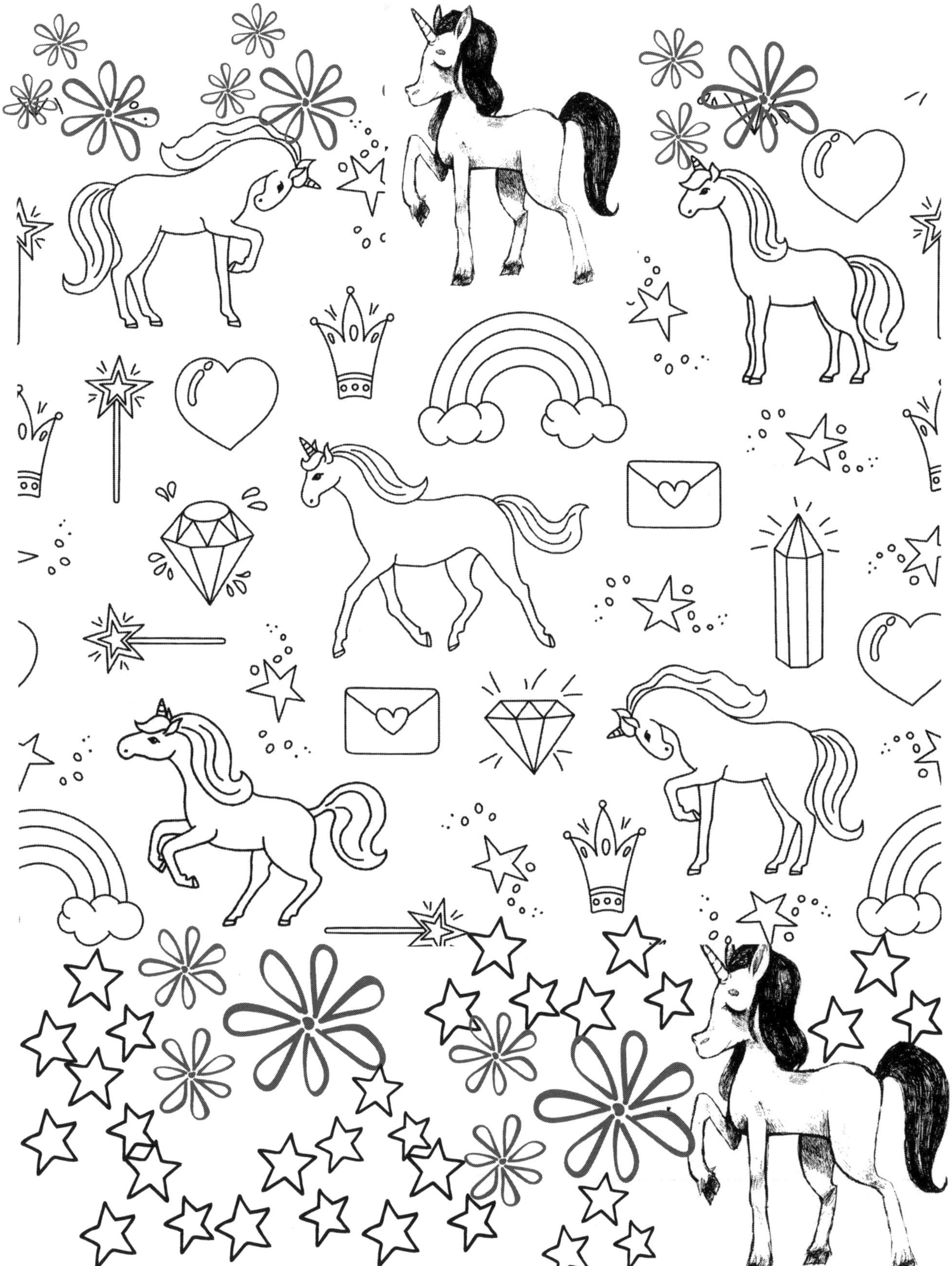

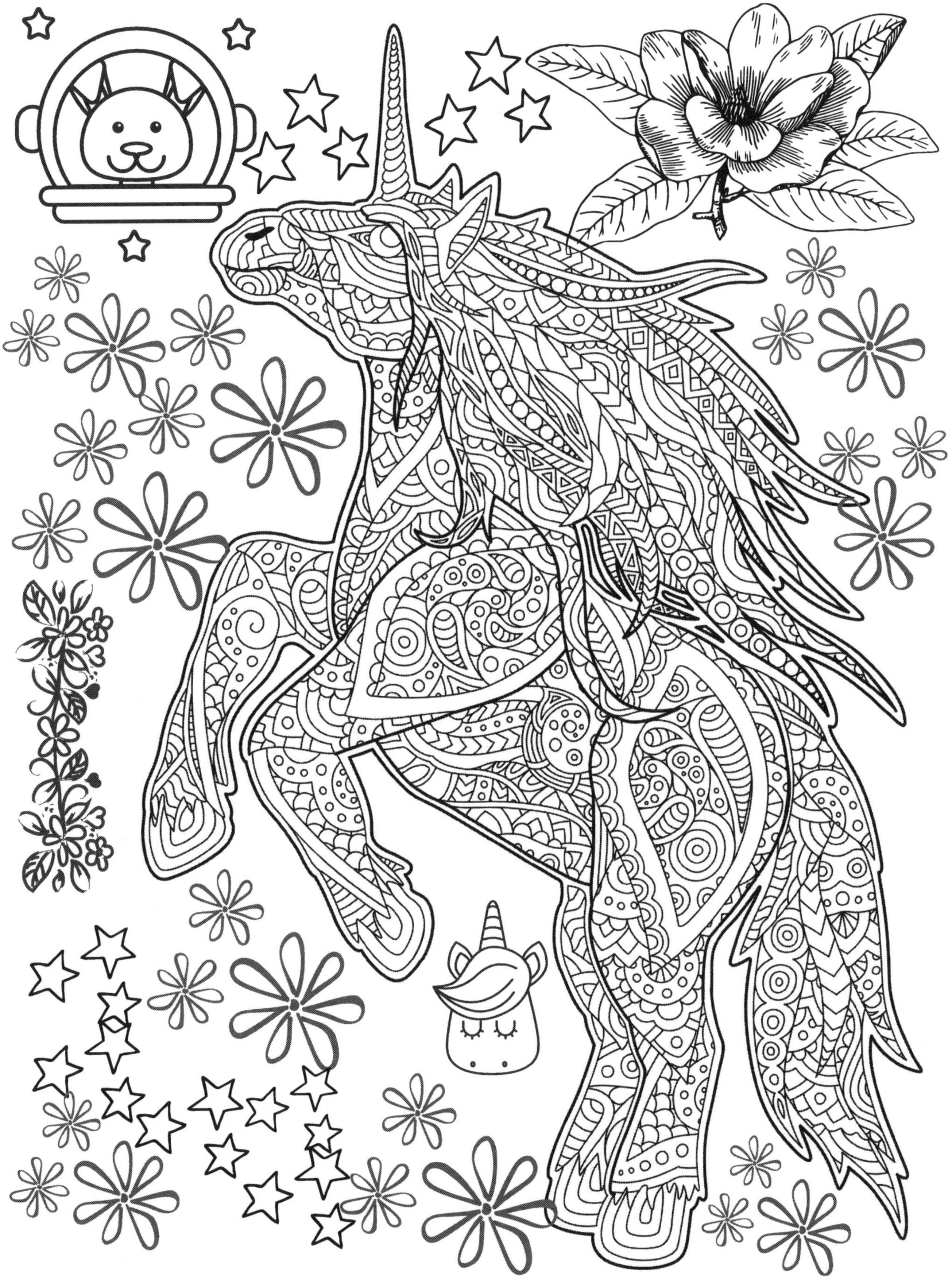

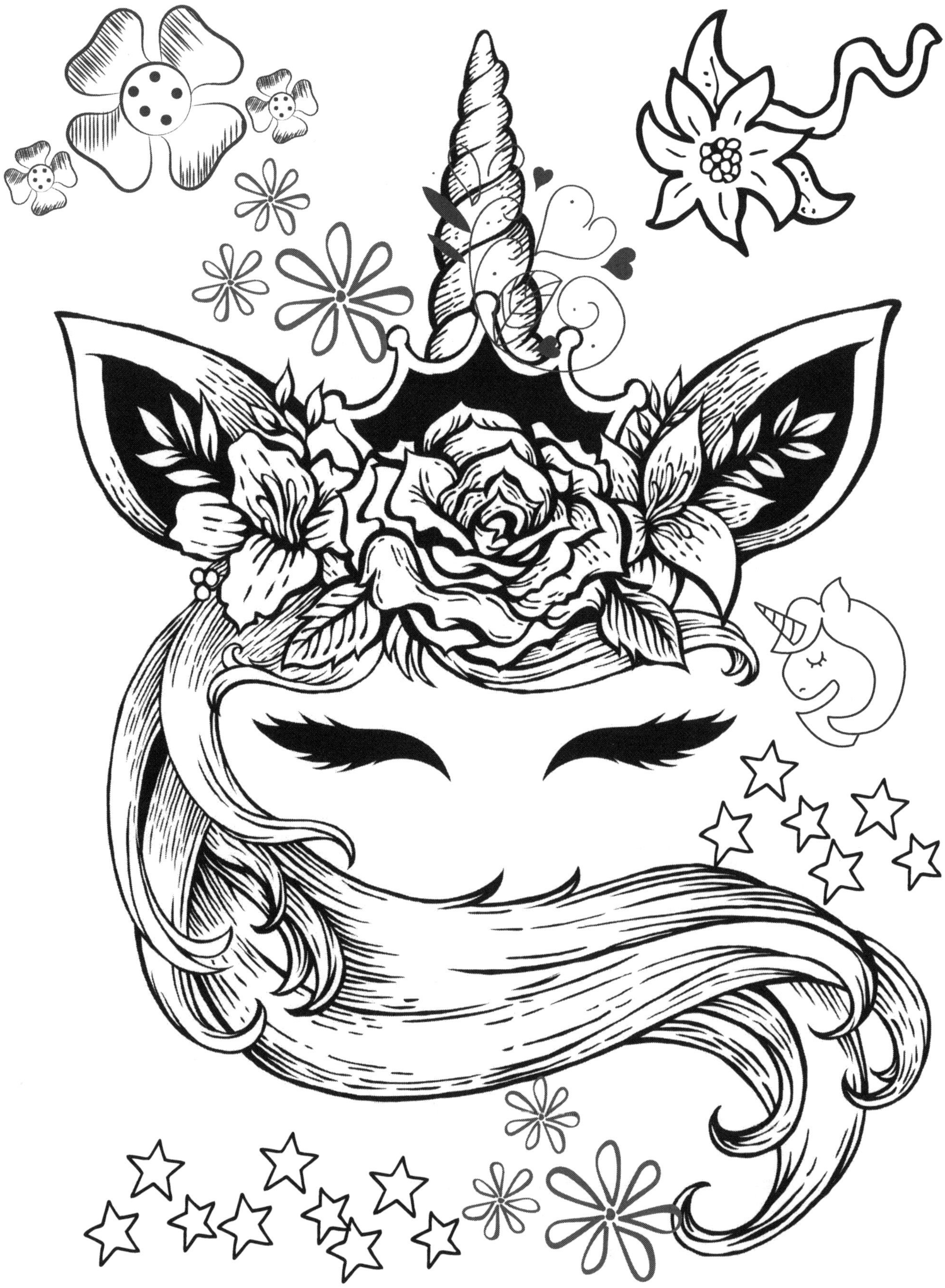

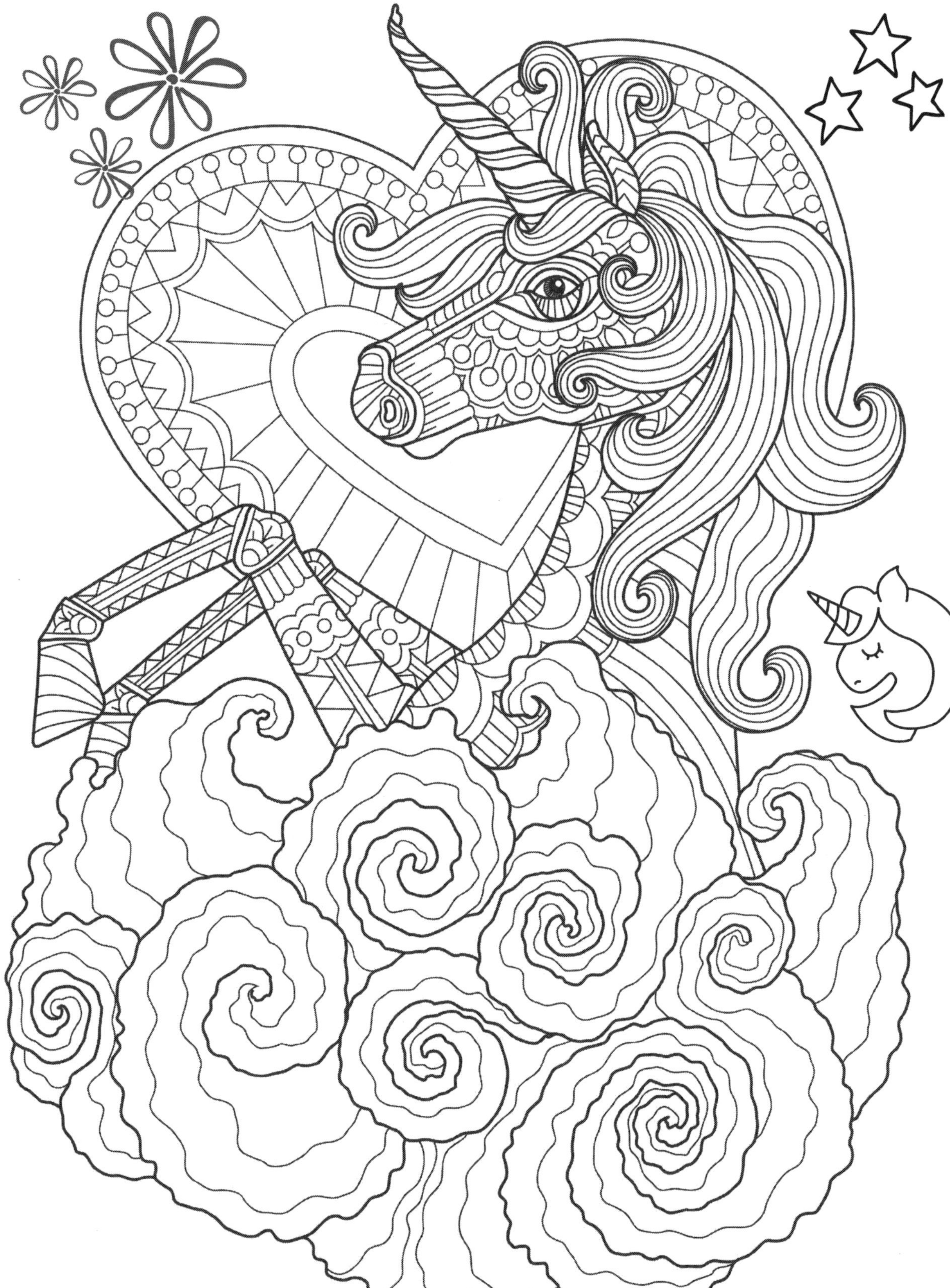

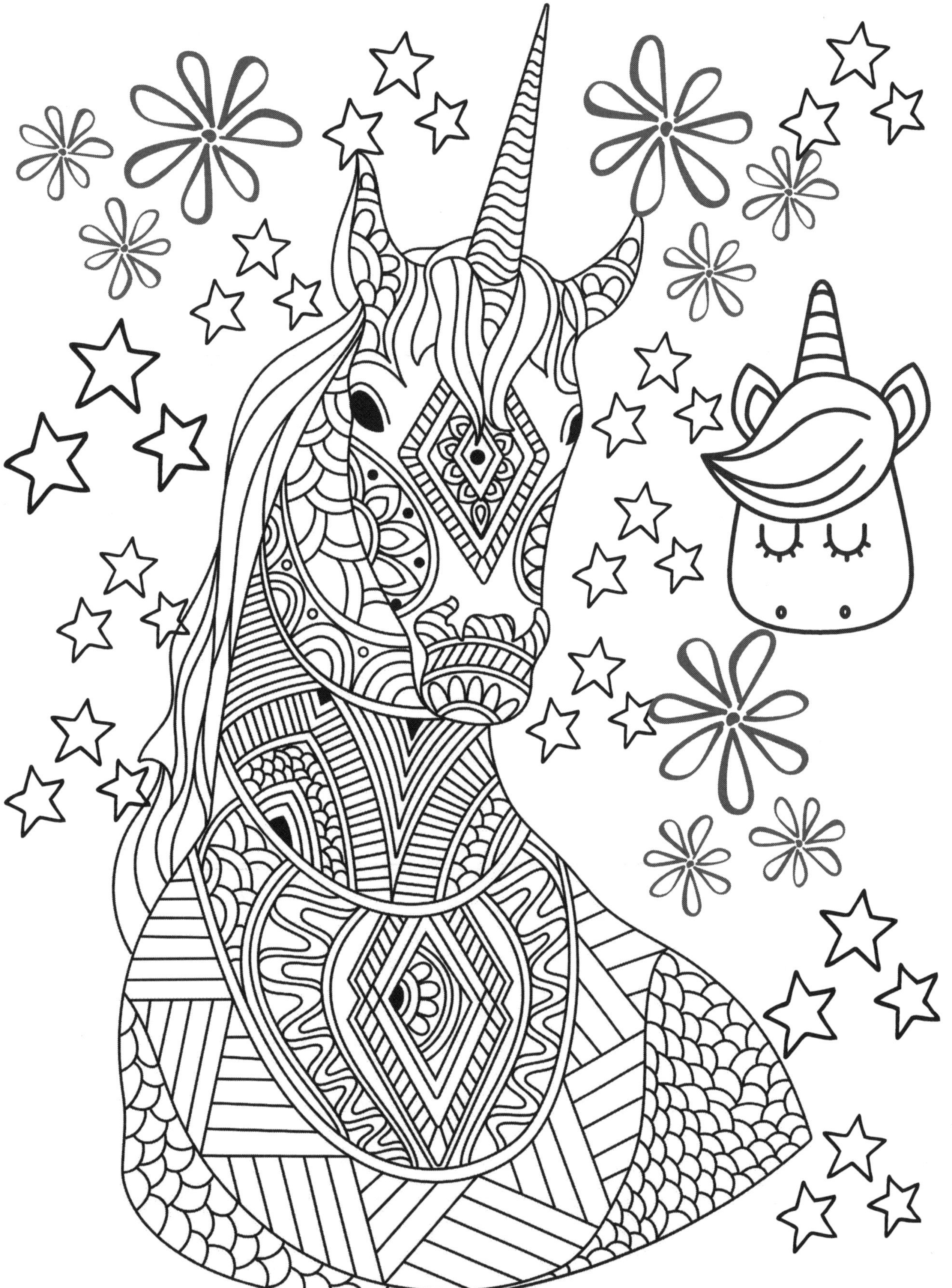

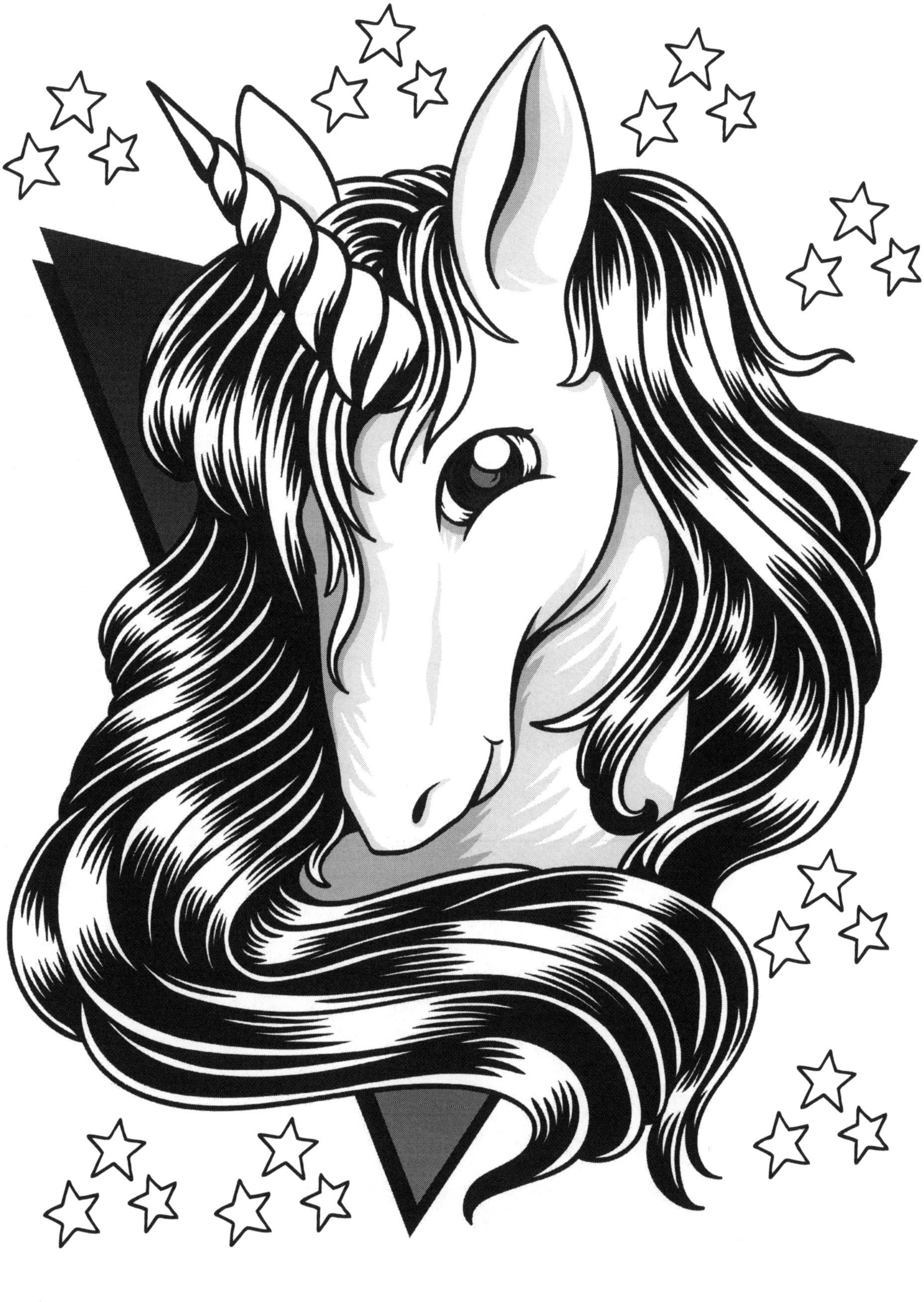

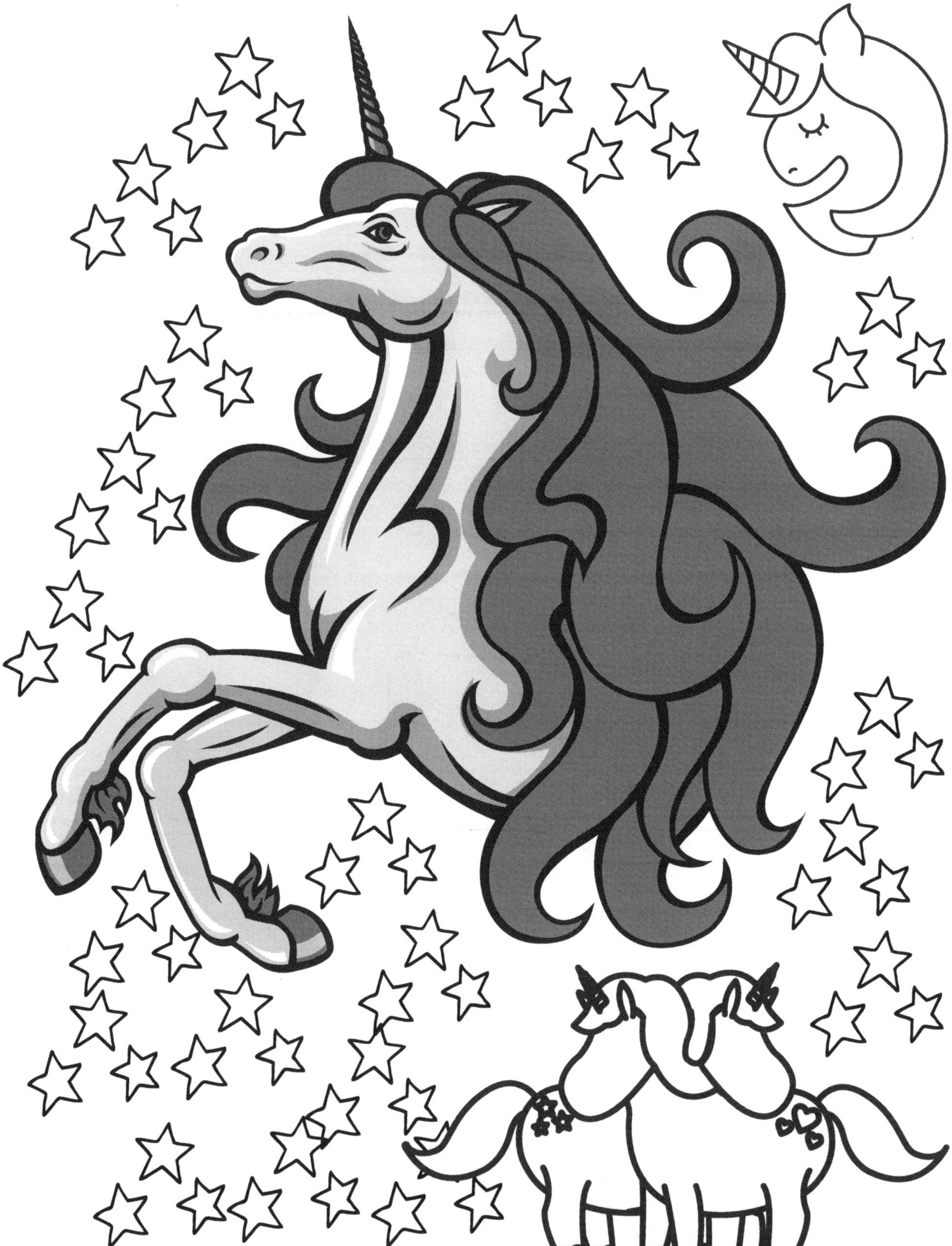

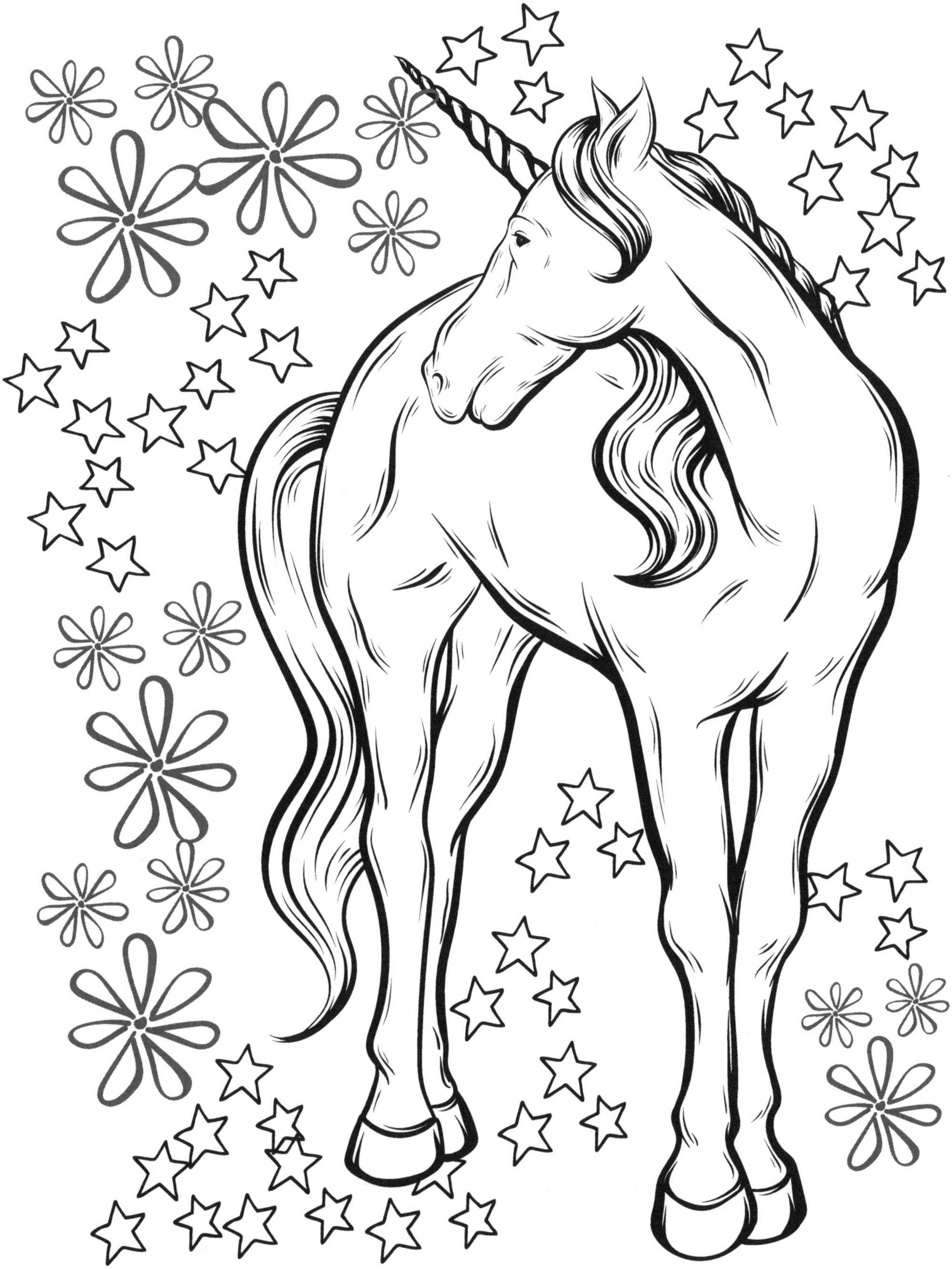

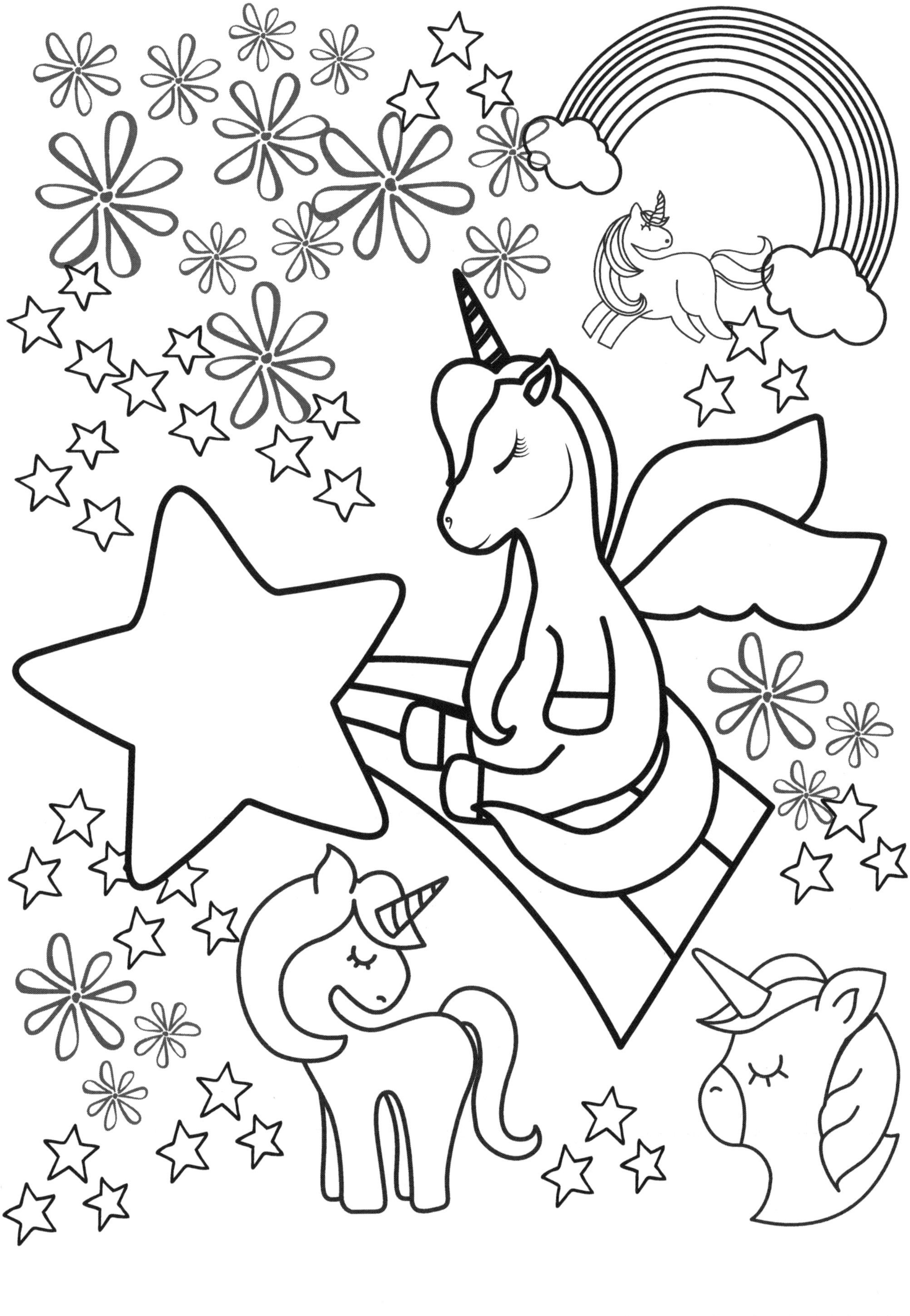

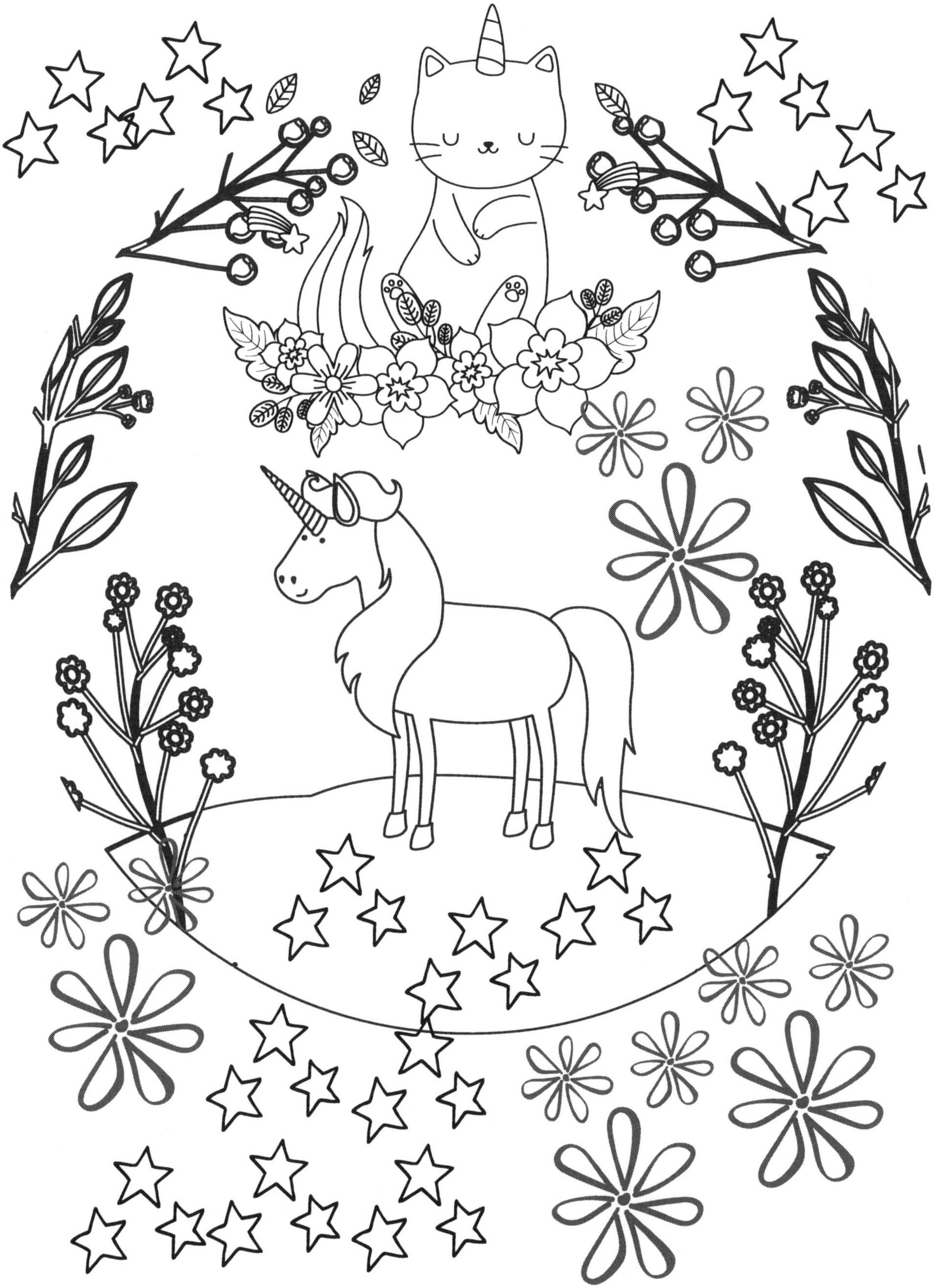

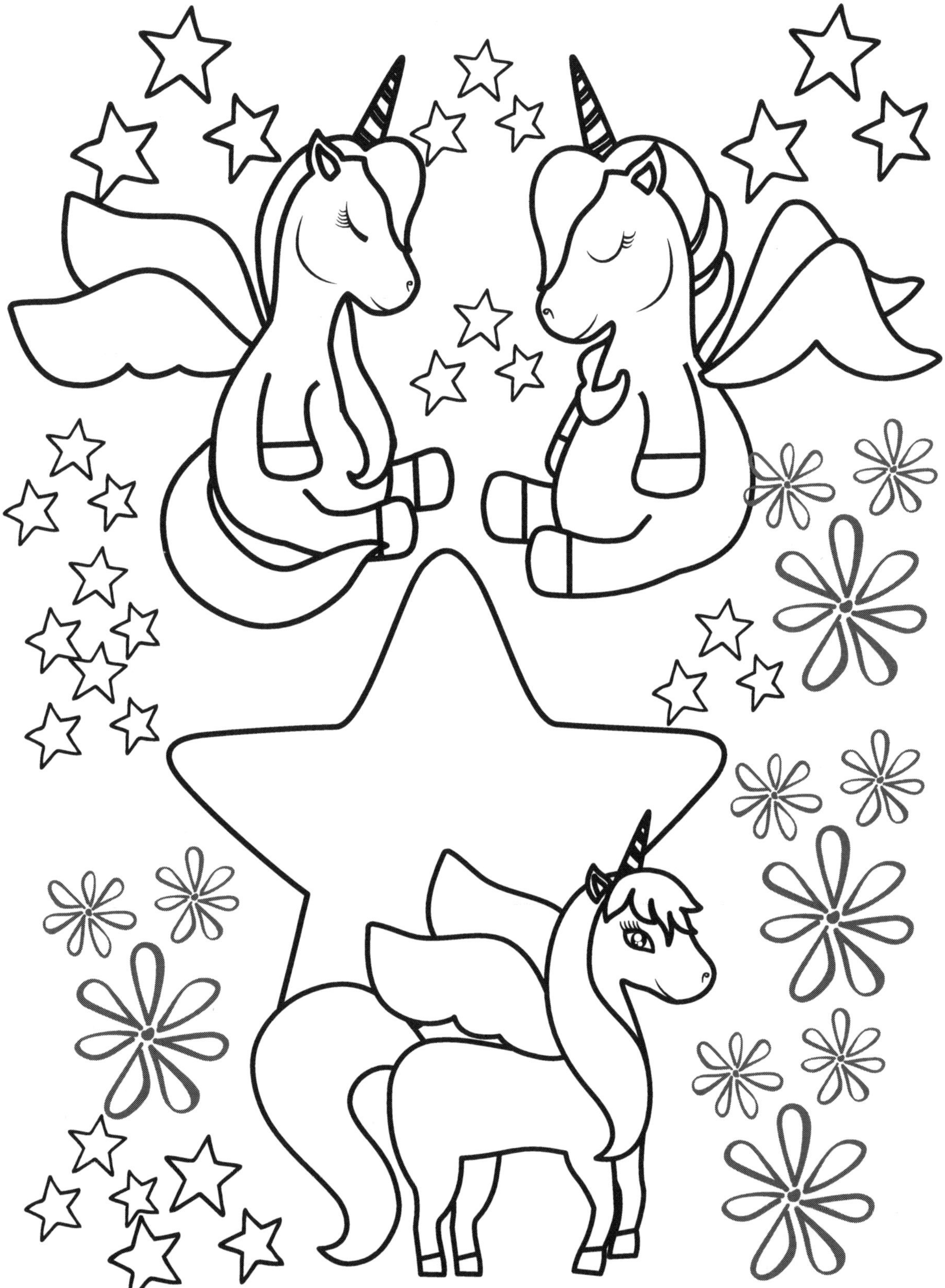

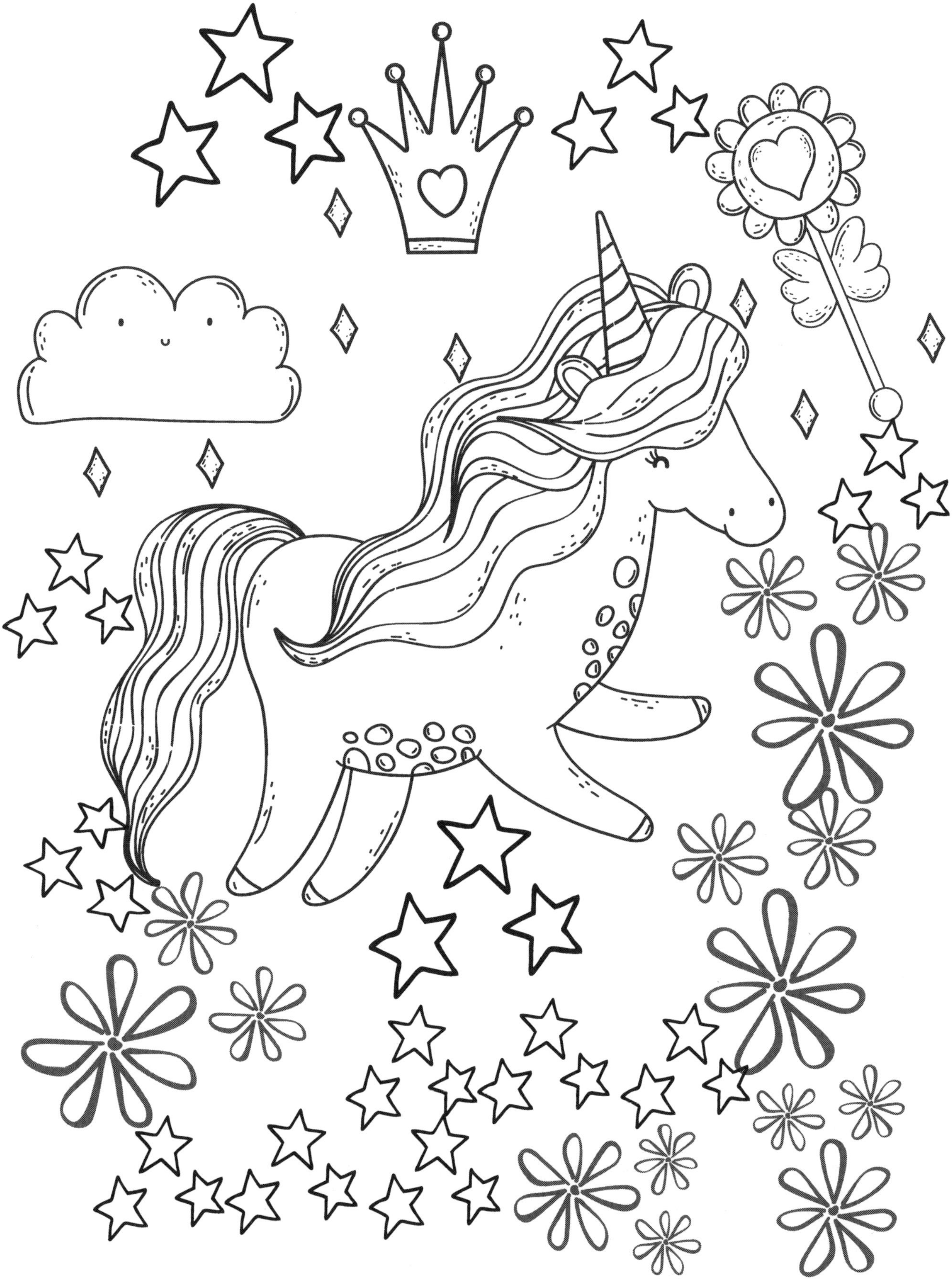

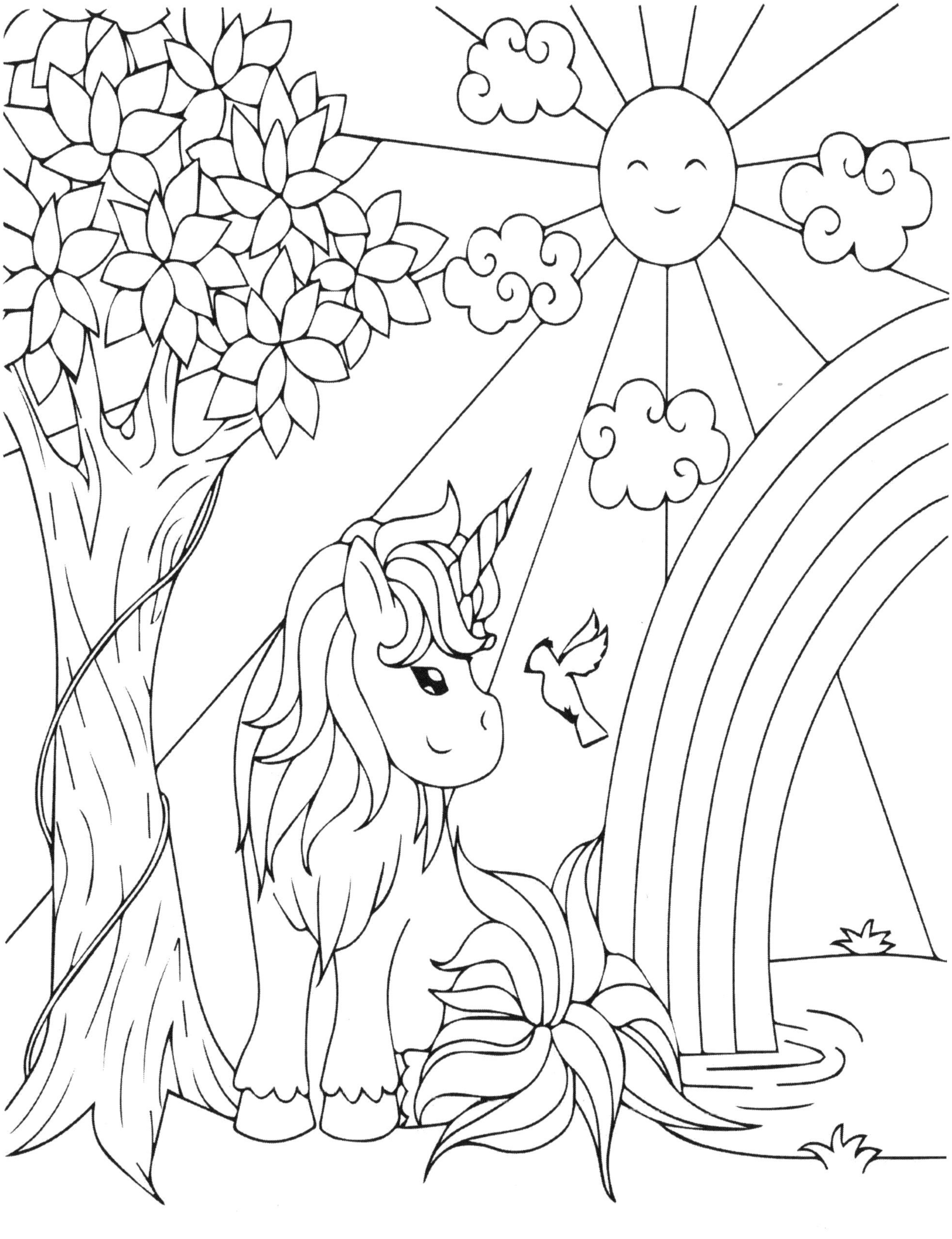

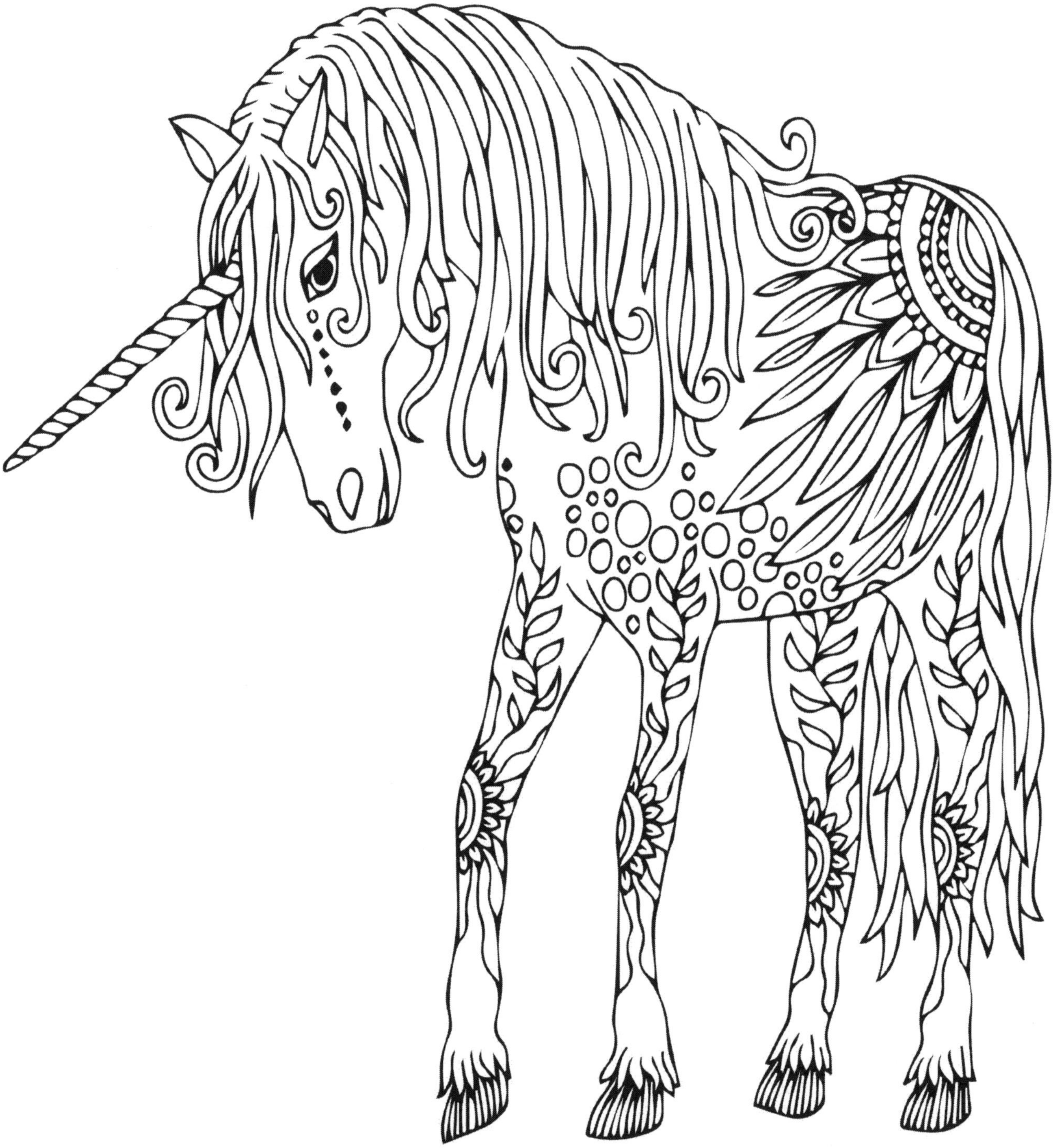

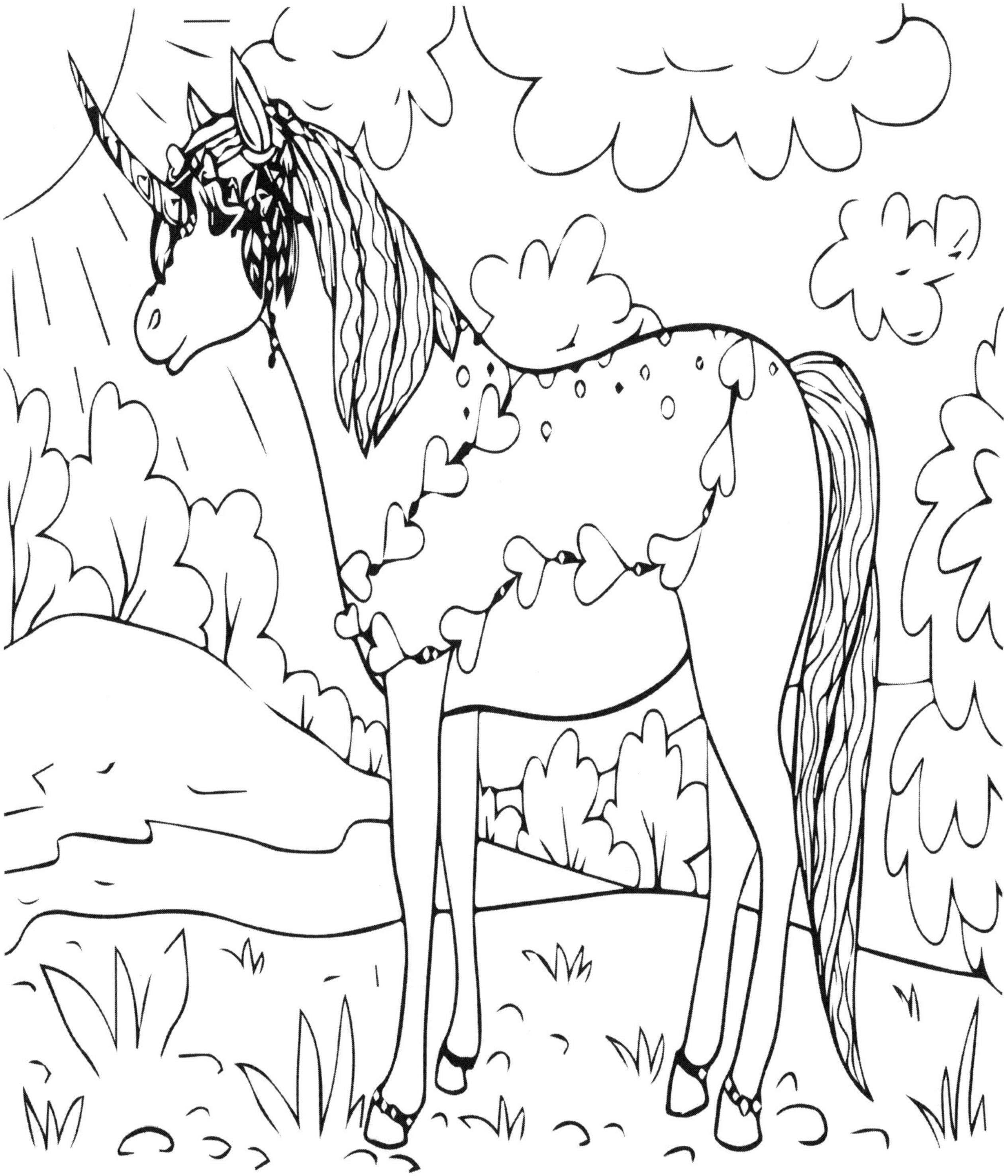

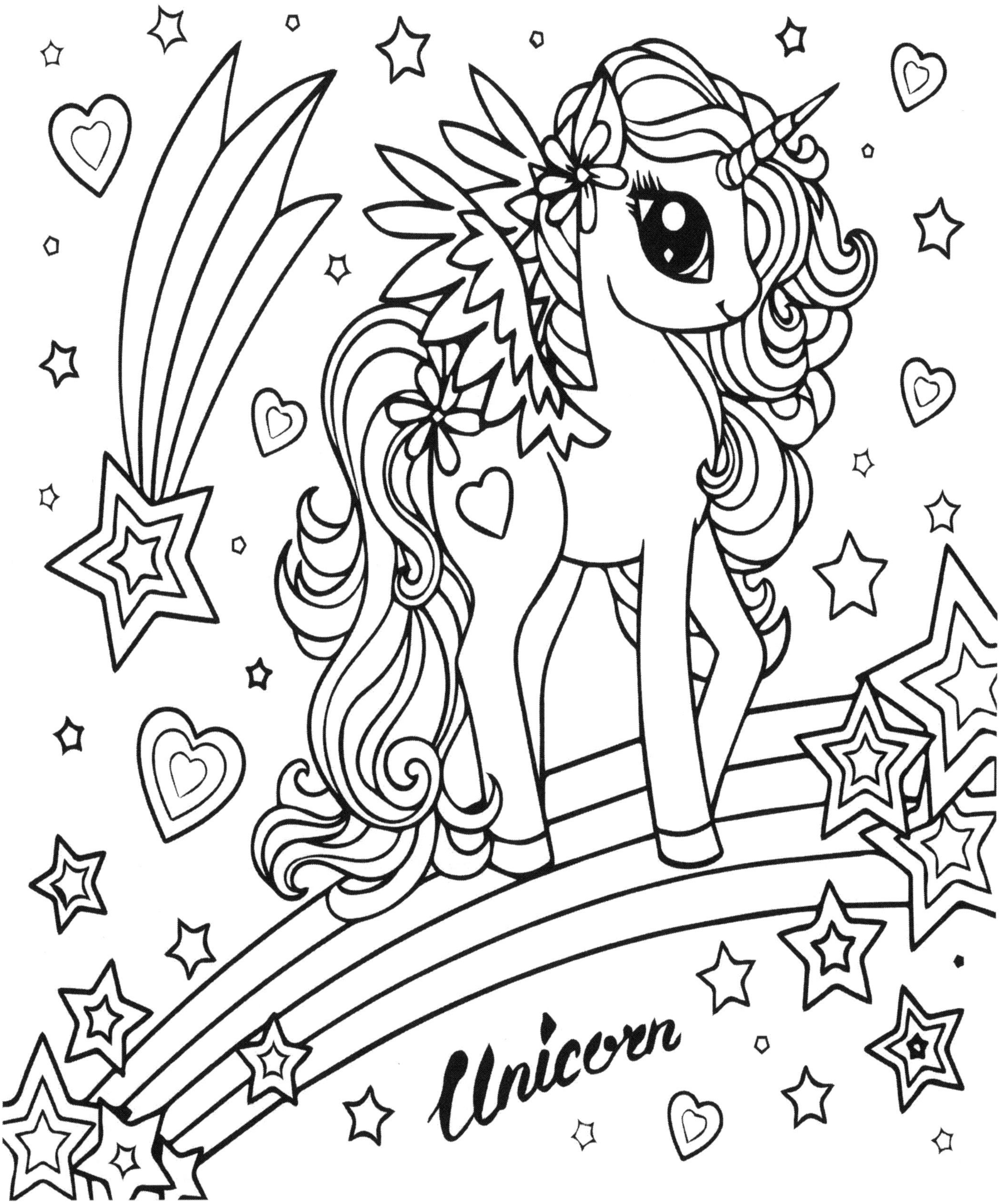
Unicorn

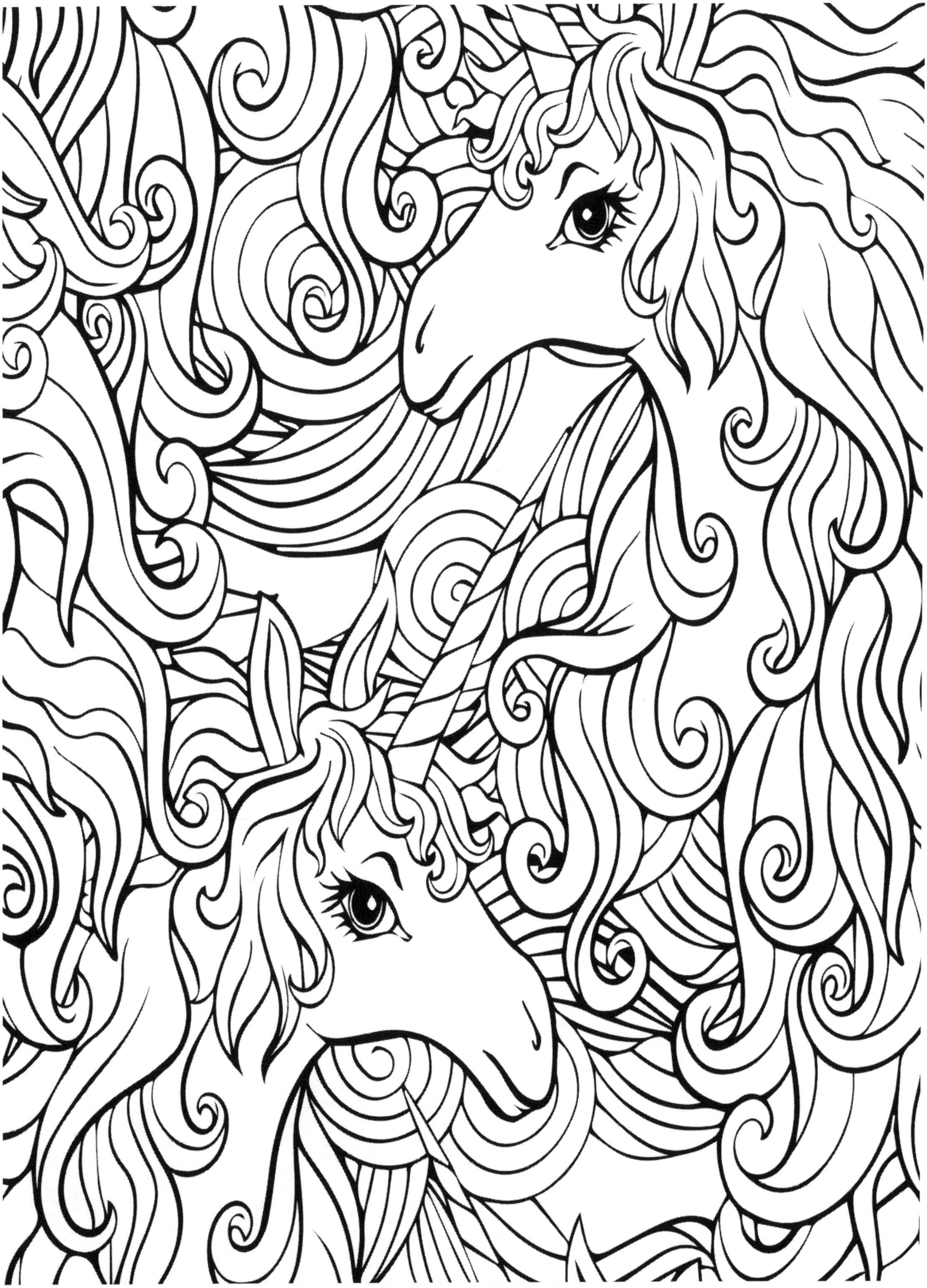

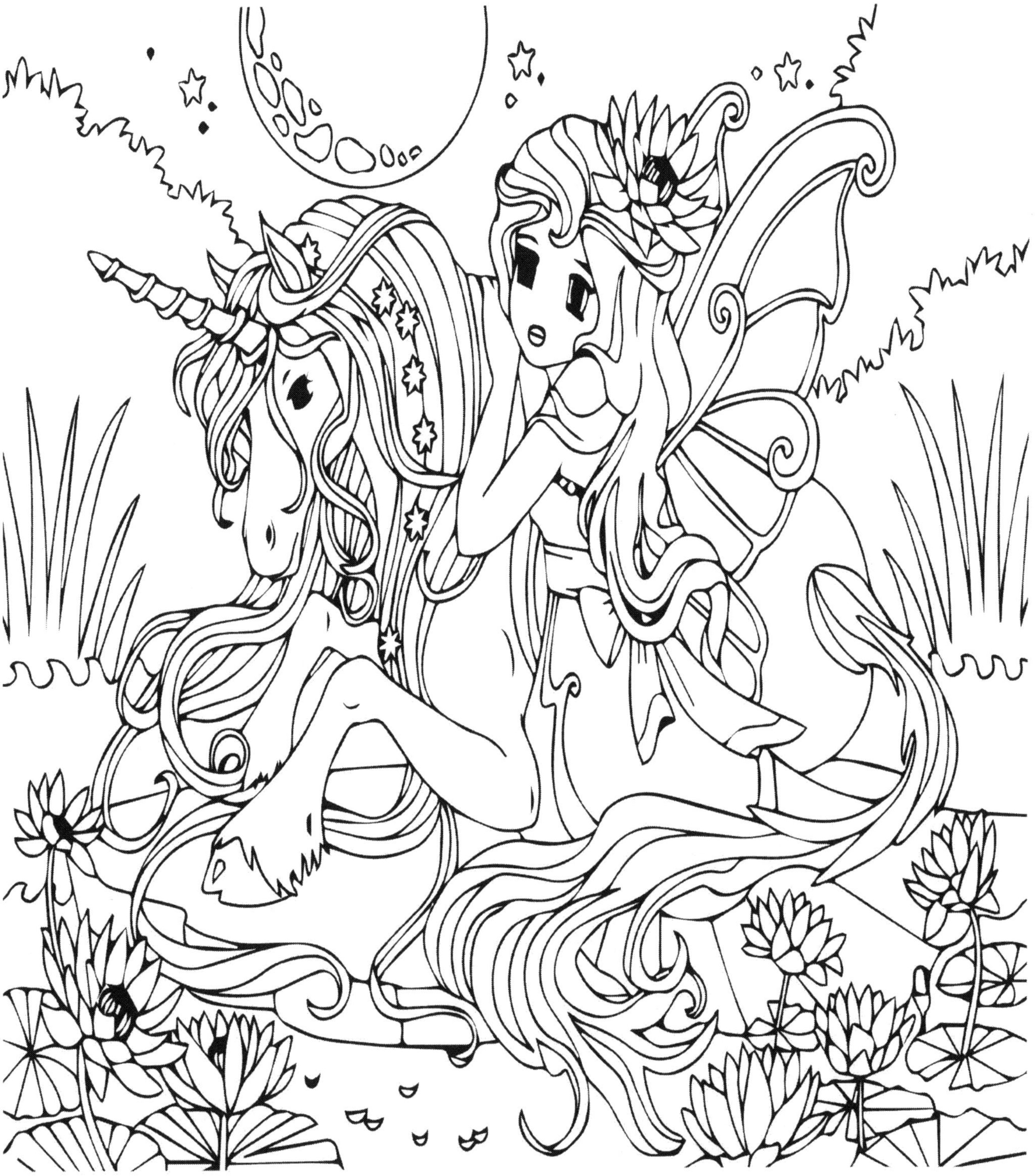

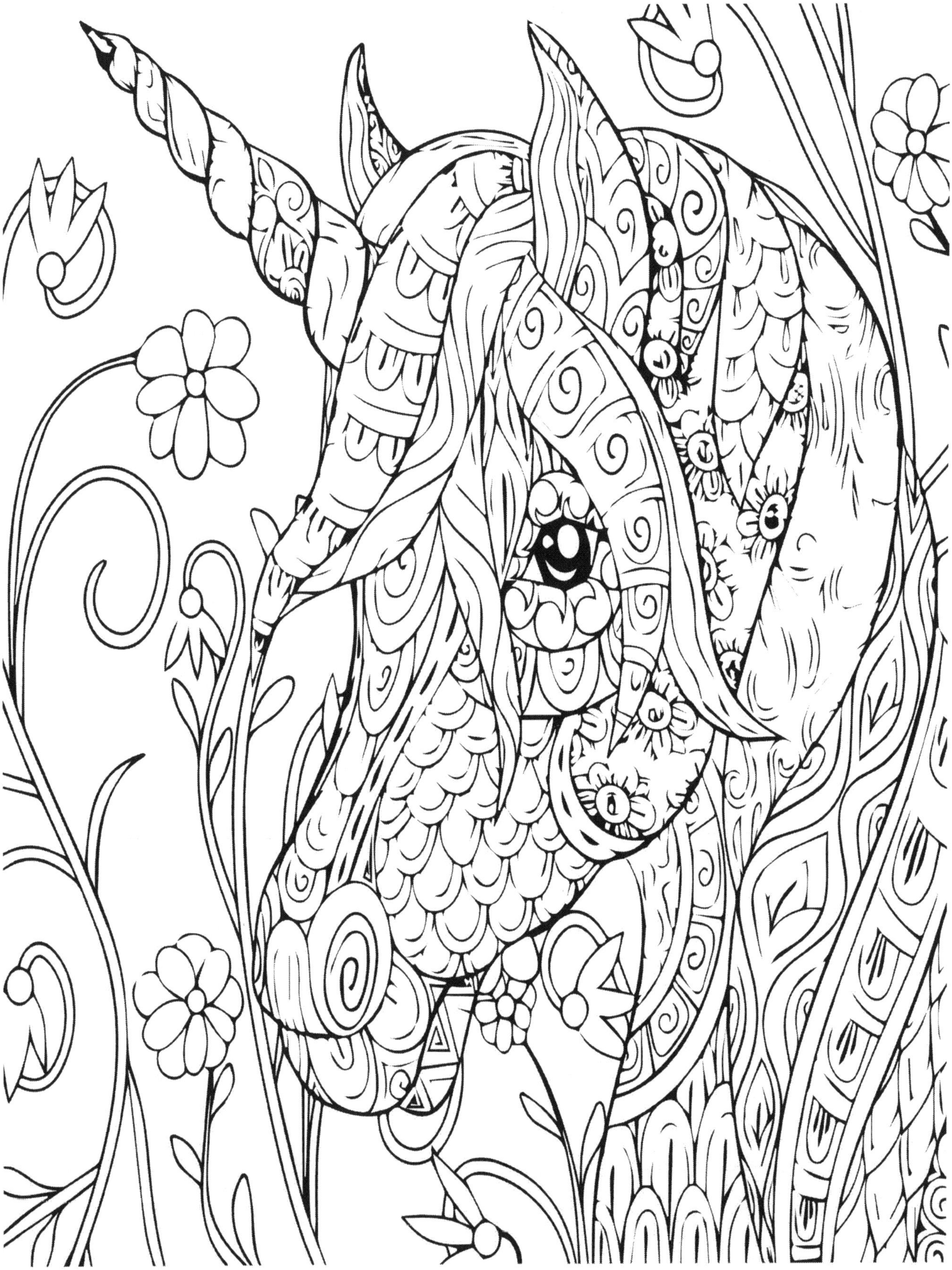

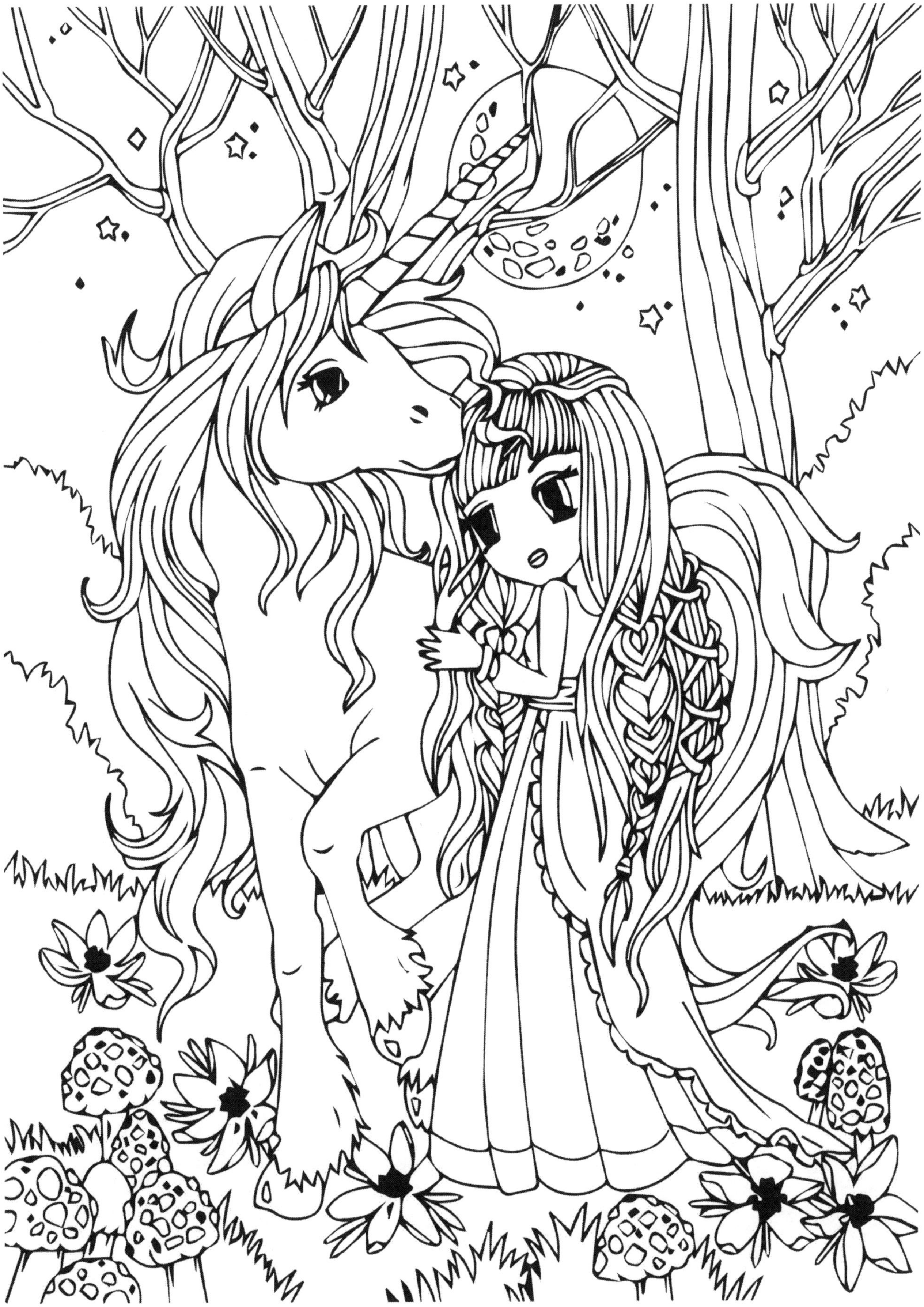

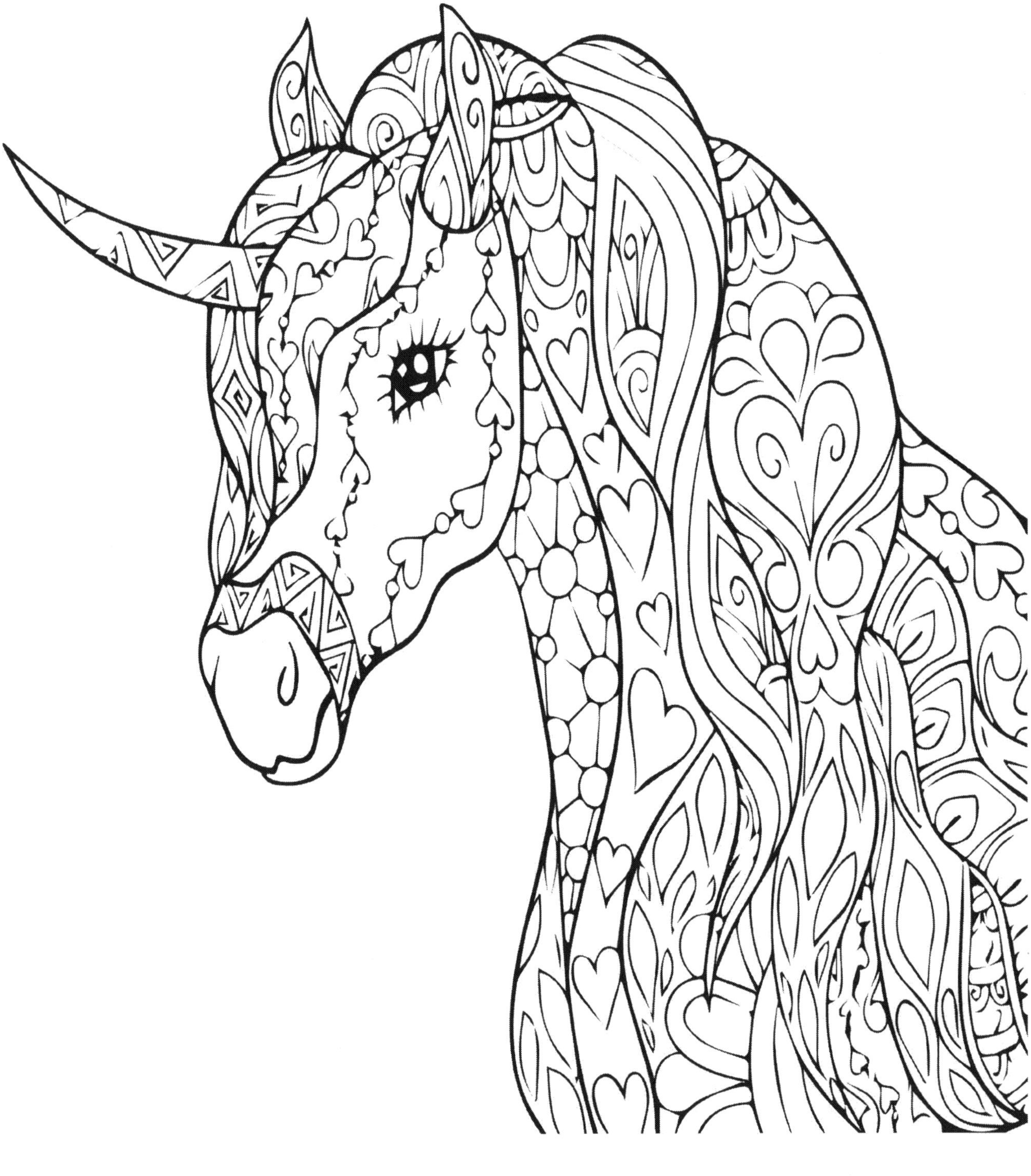

Made in the USA
Las Vegas, NV
19 July 2023

74956041R00052